After Frost

Kelley Jean White

Copyright© 2020 Kelley Jean White
ISBN: 978-93-90202-66-9

First Edition: 2020
Rs. 200/-

Cyberwit.net
HIG 45 Kaushambi Kunj, Kalindipuram
Allahabad - 211011 (U.P.) India
http://www.cyberwit.net
Tel: +(91) 9415091004 +(91) (532) 2552257
E-mail: info@cyberwit.net

No part of this book may be reproduced or transmitted in any form or by any means, electronic, mechanical, photocopying, or otherwise, without the express written consent of Kelley Jean White.

Printed at Repro India Limited.

Acknowledgments

"Adequate" was published in *Mad Poets Review*

"After Frost," "Dusk," "Presidentials," "Sweet," and "Tumblehome" were published in *The Poet's Touchstone*, Poetry Society of New Hampshire

"After the burning/the forest returns" was published in *Waterways*

"a man and child in a small canoe. . ." was published in *Heron Dance*

"Anatomical Donor" was published *The MacGuffin*

"And yet another" was accepted by *Fairfield Review*

"April Fool" was published online at *Houseboat*

"At the Weirs Beach Drive-In Theater" was published in *Abbey*

"Beached" and "Between" were published in *Illya's Honey*

"Because I loved cows" was published in *Slant*

"Belknap Mt. Road" was published in *Dakota House Poetry Journal*

"Bittersweet, " "Off Nantucket," and "The 400,000" were published *Northern New England* Review

"Black and White Rainbow" and "Darkroom" were published in *Poesy*

"Blaze," "Landscape," and "Meeting for Worship" were published in *The Taj Mahal Journal*

"Blessed" and "The Jar" were published in *Schuylkill Valley Journal of the Arts*

"Blind" was published in *Alive Now*

"Body of Water" was published in *Pegasus*

"Breaking News (The Great Stone Face has Collapsed!) was published in

The Cape Rock

"Bulb" was published in *Poetry Depth Quarterly*

"The Buzz of the Meadow, the Bees" was published in *Cider Press Review* and online at *Silver Birch Press*

"Catch" was published in a slightly different version in *Twilight Ending*

"Comes a green calm" was accepted for publication by *Azalea Plush*

"Contained" was accepted for publication by *Regenerations* and *Wilderness House Literary* Review

"Cover" appeared in *Limestone Circle*

"Crawford" was published in *Upstreet*

"Dear Peach Tree," appeared online at *Tin Lustre Mobile*

"Deepening" and "Departed" were published in *The Comstock Review*

"The Demise of the Pay Phone at the Gilford Village Store" and "Ray at Town Hall knows a lot about payphones." appeared online at *Camel Saloon*

"'Doc'," in a slightly different version, "Downhill" and "The Gilford Community Band Concert" appeared online at *Fullosia Press*

"Doublewide," "Right after I won second place for the state of New Hampshire," and "Without a Clue" appeared online at *Tattoo Highway*

"Dove" appeared online at *Autumn Sky Poetry*

"Dry Fly," "Jelly Bean, three," and "Milo at the Bandstand" were published in *Dan River Anthology*

"Durer–Study for Feet of a Kneeling Apostle" was published in *Sow's Ear Poetry Review* and in the anthology THE ART OF SURVIVAL by Kings Estate Press

"8/8/02" was published in *The Other Side* and appeared in an online chapbook, *"Every poem I write for my father is called twilight,"* at *Tamaphyr Mountain Poetry,* later archived at *Origami Condom*

"Enter Herman Mudgett" was published in *The Binnacle*

"Every poem I write for my father is called twilight" appeared online at *Three Candles;* it was also Included in an exhibit at The Museum of the White Mountains and served as the title poem for an online chapbook at *Tamaphyr Mountain Poetry,* later archived at *Origami Condom,* in will also appear in an exhibit at Castle in the Clouds in Moultonborough, NH

"Fall Lambs" appeared online at *Jellyfish Whispers* and was published in the anthology *STORM CYCLE* by Kings Estate Press

"Final" was published in *Deronda Review*

"Forbidden Drive" was published in *Ibbetson Street Press*

"Forest Service" was published in *Bell's Letters Poet*

"Forsaking" was published in *Wandering Hermit Review*

"Foundation" was published in *Pralaton*

"Friend Cow" appeared online at *Eye Socket* and as an audiofile on the Broadkill Press website

"Gathered Meeting," "Golden child, Wood, Ash," and "The Pest House" appeared online at *Ken*Again*

"The Gilford Community Band Concert/July 15, 1998" and "Hiroshima Day" appeared online at *Blue Fifth Review*

"Hair Wreath, 1865" appeared online at *Concelebratory Shoehorn Review*

"Home Burial" was published in *Philadelphia Poets* and *Hard Row to Hoe*

"Honest Things" appeared online at *Red Fez*

"Hoyt Road" and "Mastery" were published in *Hard Row to Hoe*

"I am watching the sparrow" appeared online at *alittlepoetry.com*

"I cannot say how deep the snow" was published in *Sow's Ear Poetry Review*

"Improvements" and "Matins" were published in *Parting Gifts*

"In the City of Widows" was published in *Edison Literary Review*

"I step out into. . ." appeared online at *Muse Apprentice Guild*

"It was perhaps thirty-five years ago" appeared online at *2River View*

"I wanted. . ." was published in *The Storyteller, Opossum Holler Tarot, bear creek haiku* and in the *bear creek haiku* anthology and appeared online at the bear creek haiku blog

"I will find. . ." was published in *bear creek haiku*

"Jee" was published in Parnassus Literary Journal

"Johnson's" was published in *Ink, Sweat and Tears*

"June" and "Morning" were published in *Pegasus Review*

"Juniors Favorite Chocolate Cake" was published in *Children, Churches and Daddies,* and in the anthology *BENDING THE CURVE* by Scars Publications

"Just now, in the new millennium, someone has discovered" was published in *Pine Island Journal of New England Poetry* (as "Just now, in 2002, someone has discovered)

"Kneading" appeared in *Sunstone*

"The last thing my father told me" was published in *Potpourri*

"Limit" appeared online at *Poetry Webring Review*

"Lit" has been accepted for publication in *Pancakes in Heaven*

"Lumber" appeared in *Sahara*

"Marvel" appeared online at *scarstv*

"Melba may be 103" was accepted by *Mobius*

"The Murderer of Crows" was published in *PREY TELL* an anthology on behalf of Owl Moon Raptor Center

"Night Visitor" was published in *Labour of Love*

"Nursing" appeared online at *TMP Irregular*

"Off Nantucket" was published in *Northern New England Review*

"Piper" was published in *Nomad's Choir*

"Reincarnation" appeared online at *Unlikely Stories*

"Remind me to take you" appeared online in *ZeBook Zine*

"Rosary Hill" was published in *Hidden Oak*

"Round Pond" was published in *Schuylkill Valley Journal of the Arts*, and online at *Silver Birch Press* and was included in an online chapbook at *Tamaphyr Mountain Poetry*, later archived at *Origami Condom*

"The Society of the Second Coming of Christ Jesus on Earth" appeared at *Bostonpoet.com*

"So Much to Learn About a Simple Fish" was published in *Albatross*

"Stone House" was published in *Windhover*

"Stripping" appeared on the *Ibbetson Street Press* website

"Summer I Run through the Meadows and Count the Cow Pies" and "Swallows" were published in *The Eclectic Muse*

"The Sweetest Water in the World' appeared online at *The BurningWord.com* "Swing" was published in *Chaffin Journal*

"Tatting" was published in *Pennwood Review*

"To Late Afternoon Light" and "Yellow Jacket" were published in *Philadelphia Poets*

"Tune" appeared online at *Facets*

"Twilight" was published in *Footprints*

"Union" was published in a slightly different form as "The Gnats Dance" in *Twilight Ending*

"Valley Green" appeared in *Indian Ink* (Karala, India)

"Venie knew the names of apples" was included in an online chapbook at *Tamaphyr Mountain Poetry*, later archived at *Origami Condom*

"Waking to the calliope, waking to the town" was published in *Connecticut River Review*

"walking through birdsong. . ." was published in *Cotyledon*
"Was long time waitress" was published in *A New Song*
"Weeding" was accepted by *Mad Poets Review*
"What would we do without mourning" was published in *The Oak*
"Wild Root Charlie" appeared online at *Jellyfish Whispers*
"Winnipesaukee/Summer" was published in *Mid-America Poetry Review*
"Yankees" appeared in an online chapbook at *Tamaphyr Mountain Poetry*, later archived at *Origami Condom*
"The Year Turning" has been accepted to appear in *Cardinal Flower*

Contents

Body of Water 13
Adequate 14
After Frost 15
After the burning the forest returns 16
Anatomical Donor 18
And yet another 20
April Fool 21
Ascent 22
At the Weirs Beach Drive-In Theater 23
Beached 24
Because I loved cows 26
Belknap Mt. Road 28
Between 30
Bittersweet 31
Black and White Rainbow 33
Blaze 34
Blessed 36
Blind 37
Body of Water 38
Breaking News (The Great Stone Face has Collapsed!) ... 39
Bulb 40
The Buzz of the Meadow, the Bees 41
Catch 42
Comes a green calm 43
Contained 44
Cover 46
Crawford 47
Darkroom 48
Dear Peach Tree, ... 49
Deepening 50
The Demise of the Pay Phone at the Gilford Village Store ... 51

Departed 52
Forest Service 53
Development 54
"Doc" 55
Doublewide 57
Dove 59
Downhill 60
Dry Fly 61
Durer–Study for Feet of a Kneeling Apostle 62
Dusk 63
8/8/02 64
Enter Herman Mudgett 65
Every poem I write for my father is called twilight 66
Fall Lambs 67
Final 68
Forbidden Drive 69
Forest service 70
Forsaking 71
Foundation 72
Friend Cow 73
Gathered Meeting 74
The Gilford Community Band Concert 75
Golden child, Wood, Ash 80
Hair Wreath, 1865 81
Hiroshima Day 82
Home Burial 83
Honest things 84
Hoyt Road 85
I am watching the sparrow 86
I cannot say how deep the snow 87
Improvements 89
In the City of Widows the One Old Man is King 90
It was perhaps thirty-five years ago 91
Lit 92
The Jar 93

Jee	95
Jelly Bean, three	96
Johnson's	97
June	98
Junior's Favorite Chocolate Cake	99
Just now, in the new millennium, someone has discovered	100
Kneading	101
Landscape	102
The last thing my father told me:	103
Limit	104
Lit	105
Lumber	107
Marvel	108
Mastery	109
Matins	110
Meeting for Worship	111
Melba may be 103	112
Milo at the Bandstand	113
Morning	114
The Murderer of Crows	116
Night visitor	117
Nursing	118
Off Nantucket	119
The Pest House	121
Piper	123
Presidentials	124
Ray at Town Hall knows a lot about payphones.	125
Reincarnation	126
Remind me to take you	127
Right after I won second place for the state of New Hampshire in the Betty Crocker Search for the Homemaker of Tomorrow	128
Rosary Hill	129
The Sweetest Water in the World	130
Round Pond	131
The Society of the Second Coming of Christ Jesus on Earth	133

So Much to Learn About a Simple Fish	135
Stone House	136
Stripping	137
Summer I Run through the Meadows and Count the Cow Pies	139
Swallows	140
Sweet	141
The Sweetest Water in the World	142
Swing	143
Tatting	145
To Late Afternoon Light	146
Tumblehome	147
Tune	148
Twilight	149
Union	151
Valley Green	152
Venie knew the names of apples	153
Waking to the calliope, waking to the town	154
Was long time waitress	156
Weeding	157
What would we do without mourning	158
Wild Root Charlie	159
Winnipesaukee/Summer	160
Without a clue	161
Yankees	162
The Year Turning	164
Yellow Jacket	165
The 400,000	166
Fin	169

Body of Water

a man and child in a small canoe
a loon swims near
another surfaces on the far far shore

Adequate

In New Hampshire I can walk
strong and big as my shadow
into the night tree silence
and speaking wind. I can watch
my own darkness move
over dark fields and roadways,
move into it, become night
air and breathing dark. All
is well. I open to the cool stars
and let my skin sing me home.

It was the same walking night halls
in hospital through doors
that swung and whispered with
single passage. Shadow strong
and real with courage and belief;
I am in the understanding,
the clockwork memory
of this humming machine,
alive and flowing with life
my body no longer merely mine.

After Frost

I remember my father walking me on the ice
road of the brook and we did not think
of falling. We did not touch or speak. We saw
all that was beautiful and miraculous in
change: the bubble world under ice panes,
the frozen leaf, the stones that lifted
with the road's ache. We walked into a fading
sun with the pewter air of afternoon and found
we had climbed a mountain, let go of gravity
to whoop and slide to the village past farms
and broken trees and new-lit windows, cold
houses that called us to remember night.

After the burning the forest returns

—for Dr. Al Shigo, May 8, 1930-October 6, 2006

> *"Trees as a group are intelligent. Intelligence means the ability to connect information in ways that assure survival."*

past seared hemlock, split beach, scarred maple,
I am waiting by the damp places for the thick amazement
of berries, brave through the squalling mosquito clouds,
the tearing tartness of red, raspberry, thick confusion, of black,
berry, hard ticking of grasshopper and bee as the sun climbs
noon through new green aspen saplings, moose
maple, stinkwood, black birch cotyledons, choke
cherry, ash, —pushing two-leaved through low growth—
creepers, princess pine, ground pine, mosses, whip fork
and broom, powder gun, hairy cap, succulent snow-
berry, wintergreen, fierce climbing snapdragon,
thrust through fecund droppings, bear, moose, deer
sign, rabbit scat, new green touch-me-not, honeysuckle,
wild grape, strangling bittersweet, and your own, your fungi,
destroying angel, puff ball, witch's butter, morel,
staghorn, in scrub brush, sumac, elderberry, in liminal
cattail, pussy willow, prickly wild rose; white light
on the ledges, the granite mountain, past tree line,
hot crow call on sunburned shoulder, cracked paper
birch, wind-burned pine in the place of eagles,
pail thump of rock blueberries in lichen dry desert
(lush moss-worlds after rain,) checkerberries, trillium, Indian
pipe, ladyslipper, one shaft of sunlight, and dark

owl-pellet damp, cool waterfall thrush; trees may not heal,
but the forest does, seeks fingerling strawberries
in low burning grass, sand tunneling bee hiss, skitter
ant, quick knee prickle through juniper sharp branches—
read the runes, beetle-track beneath bark, dragonflies
in coupled flight, ballooning spiders, sugar maples scarred
by drunk sapsuckers, and ashes, noon hot bird sky, you, rising
ash, smoke, pollen, snake in hawkgrasp, seed, falling—my
startled hand seizing all, red tipped and eager, pushing
into the heart of brambles, transfixed by thorns—
almost worth the fire, the blackened stumps

Anatomical Donor

—for Robert D. White, April 14, 1926-September 11, 1909

I thought about cutting off my little finger.
I thought about cutting my hair. I thought
of cutting off my good right arm, but how
could I give it to you?

I remembered the day they cut off the heads
of the cadavers, how certain people protested,
how certain others got sick. Some thought
it was a desecration, a mutilation.

I do not remember noticing that the body
was headless when I did my careful dissection
of the brachial plexus and surely the dental
students needed the heads

to make a careful study of the teeth. You had
a bridge. Years with no decay but the calcium
washed away, the gums weakened. We worried
about the left front tooth sliding down.

In Hanover last winter the students must have
studied your facial nerve. If I went
to the memorial service at the Medical School
I could tell them how you used to put

a quarter of an orange just there under your
lips and turn to me and smile. I never asked

you to donate your bodies. I took you to
the anatomy room, my parents,

and rolled back the denim sheets to show you
the anatomy of the hand. I was bold. It was
long after we had made our first fearful hesitant
cuts into the breasts,

Skin appendages, like hair or nails, nothing
more, then the abdomens, the heavy omentums,
organs we never think about, slippery.
These I did with seriousness;

with the hands I knew joy, from the Gordian knot
of the brachial plexus to the movement of blessing
by the tendons' pull. Love. I thought about cutting off
my little finger. You gave your body to be cut.

And yet another

house of seeds, comb of new light! waiting
for fire to sow ash with greenling twigs
each perfect in its armored thorned tight fist–
to be not eaten or crushed or carried–
made to wait–ten years, more, a century
for one dry summer, week after hot week
without rainfall, thunder, even the mist
of dawn grown thinner as if it wearied
of making dew drops–in just this weather
at last comes the lightning, it strikes the hearts
of trees, a forest burning, jumping sparks,
flames writing wisdom against the heavens–
we cannot read it, but the pinecones know:
they explode in heat–seed–new forests grow.

April Fool

'So I'm a widow,' she's drying her hands
on her smock, then she's back to counting pills,
'damn fool drove his truck out to the bob house,
had a few beers, headed back in 'bout ten. . .
drove right off the ice into new open
water—and wouldn't you know it, the louse
got a window open, pushed off the sill,
headed for green moonlight, crawled out on hands
and knees (cop saw him from shore,) wobbled, dove
back in. Seems he forgot his keys, wallet,
lighter, hat, some such stupid thing he had
to have. . .We weren't living together, bad
timing, for that dumb bitch he got pregnant.'
She tightens the lid. 'Insurance's mine, love.'

Ascent

my knees bruise
on sharp granite edges

remember the place
where the trail goes to soft fern and gentle pine
and always the sky grows bluer and cooler

until there is silence
and raptors on the wind

At the Weirs Beach Drive-In Theater

same spider, same web
after more than forty years
in the ladies' room

Beached

I pursue the mutilated
seagull, my offering,
a white powdered donut.
I need to isolate
him from the others;
a fight over food will risk
more ripping, more

pain. I am not fond
of seagulls but this one
holds himself upright.
A proud fan of broken
feathers sweeps the ground
behind him in a twisted curl.
He does not come

to me. He looks intently
at my hands, touches
the pieces I have tossed
with the tip of his beak.
I hope hunger is
satisfied. He walks
to the bushes where

the children stoned him
yesterday. Brian, soon to enter
seventh grade, watches.
His fist closes
around a stone.

Our town is in the news.
A boy just Brian's age

had his throat
cut at the railroad
trestle. His $200 bike
was stolen. His stepfather
found the body. I have left
the city for country quiet,
sanctuary for me and my

children. Refuge. Asylum.
Safe Harbor. No.
There are knives are here.

Because I loved cows

When I nursed my firstborn in the Arboretum
I did not face the swanboats, I did not face
the great glass conservatory. I chose a meadow
with a herd of plywood cows. I wanted

a cow on my own lawn. I remembered cows,
the great snuffling noses bigger than my two
lifted palms, the humble eyes, the hard-soft
mossy rock where the horns had been

cropped. I wanted a cow that would answer
to her name. So we went to Lancaster, rented
a little stone house fixed-up to raise a bit of money
for the real farm next door. My husband read

his journals. I held my daughter up
to pat the heifers and at six each evening
we followed the quiet Mennonite through the rows
of calm mothers. My husband paid

attention to the careful cleaning of each
teat. I pulsed to the steady thrum and piston
tug of the stainless steel machines. I was pleased
to see each cow did have a name, "Floss,"

and "Ethel," "Strawberry" and "Jane."
My city husband did not believe that the farmer
would rise to this again at six am. I knew.
But my husband would not trust

my knowing. We came back
with the second baby. Never with the third.
My husband had lost interest
in cows. By then I wanted oxen.

Belknap Mt. Road

In my town
the mailman leaves pots of herbs from his greenhouse
in the battered mailbox.
He props up the little broken flag.
He knows if you're home
or gone away to school or looking
for work.(Then he gives the letters
to your mother or your friend.)
Schoolchildren walk
at 7:40 and 3:10 past my house.
They stop at the little store
(closed only once in one hundred and eighty
years) for tootsie rolls and popsicles. Boys
do tricks on bicycles.
People bring pies door to door.
We go to the ice cream social
at the library.
We bring our books
back on time. If we forget
the librarian renews them anyway.
She knows my children's hobbies
and recognizes their best friend's mother's
car. The police car
stops children and gives them tickets
good for an ice cream cone at the dairy bar
when they wear their bicycle helmets.
The man at the store wraps up an extra
donut. You can take it to the bench
behind the children's room

at the library and listen to
the brook. People wave
at you when you walk home.
It my town everybody
knows my parents and asks
after my family's health.
I know their children
and remember their birthdays
and anniversaries
and how they take
their coffee. Only problem is
I don't live there anymore.

Between

Charlie saw it first: loud, gangling
arms pumping, too much noise, yet
he knew it to be a wonder, called,
"Miss Kelley, Miss Kelley," and I
pulled all the children with me to see;
how could he have known that I had
longed for just this, this bright ooze
dripping from fence rail to fence rail,
nearly phosphorescent in daylight,
this fragile small alien, moving among
us. Slime. Mold. Neither plant nor
animal, a community of being, bound
by salt and mute electricity, to erect
a miniature city by dawn, towers, globes,
thrust from the gray lunar landscape,
dry wood. Fool, I take a penknife,
cut a six inch piece of fence. Morning,
colors dull, dry, powder, flaking, not
much for the science room to see.
Why grasp at wonder?

Bittersweet

—for Lavenia Cole Outwater

I find it near the end of the path—
orange-red brilliant berries
among leaves
not quite
fallen:

A thing of brief, odd beauty,
it lives only by the compromise of other life.

You disparage metaphor.

So look.
Go see:

all life—
takes, uses, changes,
abuses other life,
wraps around, leans upon the other,
twists its branches,
strains its limbs,
climbing
toward the light;
falls,
relinquishes its hold,
grasping and grasped,
sustenance and sustained.

The berries are poisonous,
but something feeds here.
See, the cracked yellow shells:
Bitter.
Sweet.

Remember:
the observer changes the observed.

Black and White Rainbow

I hold a picture with scalloped edges,
yellow at the corners where I pried it
from the album's gummed triangles:
my father, strong, athletic, grinning
like an eagle scout under a thick black crew cut
and me, skinny and pale, my hair a white blur,
squinting into the sunlight. Our outstretched
arms do not quite encompass the week's catch
laid out on an island of damp newspapers
on the grass. A great fish, a rainbow trout,
lays at the top of the school like a roof beam,
the carpenters' ruler unclicked to a yard and
measuring just past its length. Forty years later
we are a negative of the shot: my hair dark,
my body heavy, my father's hair white and soft,
his arms and legs wasted, his face twisted in, closed;
still, the bristle of his unshaved chin on my cheek
tells me I'm his child and one of us
has come home from the woods.

Blaze

I take safe paths
looking for beauty;
my friend
does not follow trails.

He has taught himself

to walk through
trailless places
moving steadily ahead
on long legs.

Sometimes I have seen
my way clear to follow him,
knowing there will be difficulties,
thorns, twisted ankles,
falls, scraped knees,
and that my progress will be slower,
holding him back.

I have kept up for short distances
then accepted my limitations,
returning to the path

He has chosen, has accepted
the responsibility of maintaining
paths for others.
He keeps sharp knives
to cut away, trim back, open. . .

I caution the children
not to leave the path.
Things may be broken,
disturbed, bruised
beneath a heel, changed.

Even steps chosen carefully,
taken with care,
may damage.

He teaches them to sharpen
knives.

Blessed

a barn is a kind of church
each cow kneeling in her stall
soft lips mumbling the humble prayer of cud
the sacrament of grass turned milk and flesh
whispered ministry of tail swish dung and piss
silo reaching for the blessing of hay and oat
liturgy of flies buzzing around heavy-lashed solemn eyes
dim light transfigured through unwashed windows
hands face hair kissed by cobwebbed dust
heartbeats tuned to the brass note of the milking machine
and a solemn soloist a trumpet lowing
bodies shifting in the hay-sweet breath
supplication of dappled light and calm domestic power
heavy tongues lapping offered salt and grain
we lay our nickels on the cool granite table
in the chapel of the milk room
bottles filled with essence of soul and sweet clover
sunlight meadow flower and swift singing brook

Blind

—for Edith Kelley Outwater

Light wasn't needed. You could touch the dark,
find your way with a fingertip and pass through.
Blinds drawn, she rocked near the doorway,
scant white hair, gaunt face, blue white eyes,
the ivory cold hands wanting to hold ours,
and they did, and we heard all the stories from
the McGuffey's reader of 1863, stories about boys
with short coats and long scarves falling through
the ice, girls tearing their skirts on berry bushes,
faithful dogs, lost chickens, spelling medals,
cold hearths, war. I had a Liberty half dollar
she had closed in my hand, as old as the Civil War,
as old as Edie, its strong narrow woman striding,
a warrior, Edie's gift, and I carried her name.

Body of Water

Any pond or lake in New Hampshire will
do. Or Maine, or Vermont, or upper New
York state; anywhere in the North Country,
really. Silhouette a man in a canoe
with a trout rod against the setting sun.
Make it as colorful as you want, glorious
reds and oranges, lavender, mauve,
or choose that moment when the colors
have already gone. It should be quiet
so you can imagine the almost unheard
plink as the fly hits the water, the silent
movement of the wrist, the whisper
as the line is played out. There. You know
what the hat looks like, how it shadows
the face. You know the band of dry flies
stuck to sheepskin. The vest. The water
bottle. The cushion below the knee.
The paddle laid aside in careful readiness.
The snap-metal box of flies. All this
you know all this. You have seen my father.

Breaking News (The Great Stone Face has Collapsed!)

–after Frank O'Hara

The Old Man of the Mountains has collapsed!
I was driving along and suddenly
the radio started squawking and staticking
and you said it was the oldies station
but the oldies don't hit you on the head
hard so it was really alternative rock and
static and I was in such a hurry
to get you to McDonald's but the traffic
was acting just like the radio
and suddenly I hear the DJ
THE GREAT STONE FACE HAS COLLAPSED!
there is no radio in the White Mountains
there is no static in New Hampshire
I have seen a lot of mountains and a lot of men
and some of them acted perfectly disgraceful
but they never actually collapsed
oh Great Stone Face we love you get up

Bulb

I've spent my brooding winter underground;
today I lick my stiff gray fingers green,
my slow veins pulse unevenly, a song
I've never sung, I cannot find the words
my voice a cracking shell, it will be stirred
for prayer or praise. I know where I belong,
to some new choir, my ears grown squeaky clean,
and now unstopped from mud, they hear the sounds
of marsh and brackish water, I'm serene
with waking, and I've learned to thirst for light,
and unexpected stretching out for heat.
I can't pull back, my face is seeking air.
It wants now to unfold, open to sight.
Yet part of me is asking to retreat
to soil and cold but life would have me near.

The Buzz of the Meadow, the Bees

There was supposed to be a horse,
and my pockets full with imagined sugar;
he would lean his quiet head to me; I'd pull
armfuls of apple blossoms from the trees and braid
garlands for us both; and there'd be apples too,
a tree full of apples and flowers, apples to share
with his gentle velvet lips and I would climb
upon his back, my hair a yellow curtain; we'd ride, sing,
let him be golden in the sun,
let him be silver in moonlight,
let us leave earth and climb the arch
of the milky way, sweet flowering planet,
your cool dark sky. But I am a small child.
No horse has come to the fence. It is cold at night.
My pockets are empty.

Catch

you know that light
that evening light
when the crows call out
to one another and bend
the topmost branches of the empty trees
and it might be the end
of the world
and it might be a blessing
and it might just be
a promise
that you call me to see

Comes a green calm

woods heavy with rain
fragrant:
ferns
we crushed
to make our beds

Contained

Into the box I fold my father's merit badge sash, brown, each patch hand
sewn in red thread, the eagle medal pinned with care;
I tuck in a picture of my mother, nineteen, sunbathing on a rock, arms elbows out
 behind her head, pin-up perfect,
I slide in the card-bound journal my father kept at sixteen: at sea, at sea,
20 men killed, at sea, at sea. It fits exactly against the back of the box;
I place another curled picture against the side: my father stands behind my mother,
holding her arms outstretched as they both bow:
 "engaged and happy," 1948.
His slide rule slips ivory smooth from its case, cool in my hand as I lay it
in the bottom of the box with money clip, trout patch, model sailboat,
IBM forty years service watch.
I unfold a brittle column of newsprint, Laconia Evening Citizen, 1956,
"Bob White played like a firecracker," in the men's racket league,
repeat its intricate folds, secure it inside.
Next the red spiral notebook, fishing trips, 1986 to 1996, "water temp 43-45.
rises all over, 12 caught, 2 kept, laid in with care, then navy dogtags,
St. Christopher medal, scapular, and weighted down last

with the knife, dark bone handled, magic, heavy, hard,
found alone in the bottom left hand pocket of the fishing vest—
it is the last thing, I cannot let go without crying,
as the lid fits precisely, closed.

Cover

I lift a log and shock the thigmotactic world:
sow bugs scurry and roll, worms gleam
naked, vulnerable in the sun, a slug cowers
as my hand recoils, his thick body brown as
polished wood. My eyes are not fast enough
to count the scuttling lives. I am careful not to
crush the slug beneath my stone. I have made
a handsome wall. Tomato plants lean against it.
A morning glory climbs tomatoes to free air; its
tendrils search for higher sustenance. They draw
my eyes to the pear heavy with hard green fruit,
the maple dripping with seed, the taller branches
of an unknown tree. Moist wind hits my face,
clouds sprint into rain. I am a fool. I own no
umbrella or hat. My son asks if the Buddha was
the only one to reach enlightenment. I have
no answer. I cannot teach. I cannot hold or even
speak what I am become: stardust falling on
every living thing. Thigmotactic, I go inside.

Crawford

Believe what you will—the man throttled
a bear on the side of a cold winter
mountain, carried it through thigh
deep snow to his wife's fire—She cut
the frozen meat with her teeth, scraped
the hide with a curled nail, rubbed
the grease into her husband's
hair, made their skin rich with oil,
lay down in heat, a long sleep—
they drank snow, climbed the mountain
we call tall, found their new clawed
hands could hold no tool, their muzzles
did not speak—they no longer wanted
fire. Good with silence, they left
no record, went to live outside
any fellowship but their own, knowing
the true name of the mountain, waiting
for us to call it, waiting for us to call them home.

Darkroom

Our hands are brother and sister
in the pans. Yours longer, only
a little thicker, move quickly, deft,
mine, a little slower, try
to follow. Bark, ragged, torn,
heavy, emerges, the Everglades,
in shadow, and you are telling me
about its light here in the dark. I tell you
how I found a book made by
my father, photographs
and old newspaper clippings,
every report card and award and
test score I ever earned. I never knew
I say, I never knew he kept them.
I did well. You turn and take my face
for one quick moment
with those, my mated hands,
breaking our unspoken agreement
to never touch, to wait, to stay
in friendship only, then you bend
again to the work, a careful, steady man.

Dear Peach Tree,

we wanted you
to bless us
and signify flower
and fruit
good and sweetness
in growing to light

we intended
to bless you
gave you our best
dirt and a great
enough hole
and water
each day

but we have only
dull voices
and little wisdom

we call our
limits
love

Deepening

He got me. I can't beat him Indian wrestling any more, not
legs-locked elbows-hooked circle-on-the-floor;
he's chuckling, voice turning man-dark and it's not *Boys
Life* in the bathroom, it's stolen pictures under the bed
and bullets—real guns, blackened wood, rubbed steel; we won't sleep
in the dugout by the brook anymore, branches broke
with our pitch stung hands, we can't arm wrestle, his shoulder's big
as his father's and he's cut a rattlesnake tattoo. He's crossed

over. He's tricked me. He's lit a cigarette. I'm kneeling
in the snow and he's laughing: he fed me gray meat from the tip
of a knife, deer meat I swallowed and can't choke out:
I'm kneeling, praying to the carcass
strung tree to tree, gray muzzle flung back to bare
branches and a single star, kneeling with white hands
in the spitting snow, bare-headed in this church of wind.

The moon's a splinter. The brook's silenced, locked, under six inches
of ice. And he's snorting, eyes shadowing, mouth crooked
in the flare of the match. He's groaning that deep laugh, he's grown
up and I'm praying to raw ribs and the string of dark rubies
dropping on my knees and I will not forgive this boy, will not forgive
the man he will become, but I will not fight him, won't wrestle
him on pine needle or fern and I know one day
I will drink his gin and go empty
into that black cold.

The Demise of the Pay Phone at the Gilford Village Store

First, Norm said, the Pepsi truck hit it.
The phone belonged to a private company,
he didn't remember the name, They came
to fix it. Right after it was fixed, said Norm,
a plow truck hit it. Took it clean off the building.
He picked it up, put it in his back room and called
the company. He called a bunch of times.
After a few weeks gave up on them. Two years
later some guy came into the store looking
for his pay phone. Norm told him it was in the back.
He asked him why his company never returned
his phone calls. The guy looked at him and said,
'Well, we're not very good at answering the phone.'
He left. Norm never saw him or the payphone again.
Norm didn't pay for the phone and he didn't make
any money on it. It was a pain, really. Kids stuck
gum in the coin slot. Shredded the phone book.

Departed

After a line by Mary Oliver

> Cone snails, that are endangered as they live in tropical coral reefs which are being lost the world over, mainly as a result of global warming, may contain more medicines to treat human maladies than any other group of organisms.
> —Dr Eric Chivian, Center for Health and the Global Environment, Harvard Medical School

My father is gone past twilight. His memories.
His voice. That moment when he paddled silently
beneath the belly of a moose, her soft lips
dripping duckweed and waterlilies. His startled truce
with a startled bear. The fawn that drank
from his salty palm. And the loon, oh the loon diving
beneath his little canoe, long as a man, six feet and more
with neck and feet outstretched in the dark waters,
the loon that rose, that opened its elegant beak and cried out.
Life. So many things forgotten. So many things never known.
So many things lost that might have saved our lives.

Forest Service

walking through birdsong
to a white birch
I do not bend
to pick
wild strawberries

Development

They are in a doorway, but you can't tell.
Bright faces emerge out of darkness.
Plastic jewels reel down the baby's chest,
pool in her lap. (She has hung a dozen
necklaces around her neck.) One giant slipper,
out of focus, brushes the lens. She peeks
over large yellow sunglasses pulled below her eyes.
Ribbons curl over her head, beside her sister's
smile. And it is a smile. The big green shirt falls
forward, exposing a little shoulder. Dimple.
Good cheekbones. A missing tooth. Pearls
and lace. Darkness behind them. Dark
underneath. Am I behind the camera
or in the dark room behind the door?

"Doc"

-for Willis Hoyt, DPM

When I got into Harvard Medical School
Doc Hoyt got himself an appointment with the Dean,
made the trip south to Boston, asked the Dean
to suggest an appropriate book for a young woman
starting classes in September. Then he came by the house,
swung himself up on the porch, leading with
that strong big face, that slow rocking walk,
that slow heavy voice smudged
with laughter and shrewd intelligence,
held it out in those farm big hands.

I have it on my shelf now, right here in Philadelphia,
Steadman's Illustrated Medical Dictionary,
Philadelphia, where Doc studied at the College of Podiatry:
"In the years ahead when you use this
think of "Doc" Hoyt. . ." 35 years. (So far.)
Oh, I think of home. the Volunteer Marching
& Chowder Society. 'Easy Street'. The 'Foot Hospital'
that cheated the new zoning laws against business
in the village, his bench beside the brook,
the garden, the perfect woodpile
(cut round ends of logs nailed in place),
the hoax he foisted on the village library,
with neatly typed labels: *rare albino fish*
caught in Gilford Brook 6/11/98,
tied to specimens with string and
placed on display in their glass case

(look close, the scales point
in the wrong direction, the eyes
are black seeds, these are milkweed pods
doctored by hand; he always has anything
you might need .

Doublewide

Mother insisted, so after the surgery
I sit like a kid on the back steps
with the onions and winter boots
to call the two Pearls
from K-mart–
and of course they are breathless
and weeping and I know they're thinking
I'm just like their daughters, divorced,
depressed, heavy, and how
Mother worries

I'll grow up to be the crazy fat lady
with all the cats living in one room
in the big old house–but now Mother's fear
is that they'll come to visit–
and of course they do,
Big Pearl with her O2 tank
and walker, little Pearl all fidget
in yet another wedding suit
(this one, the Pink Tropic)
from QVC

and she'll talk about the wedding,
postponed again, by Carl the Butcher
she had a fling with in the sixties,
a double amputee diabetic,
his wife's dead now,
so he calls her, came to visit
but they couldn't get his wheelchair

into her trailer (Big Pearl whispers
she wouldn't hold her breath
on building the ramp)

but little Pearl's made room
in the closet, bought a Queen
size bed and I'm thinking how you called
me after twenty-three years
surprised to like me
more now than that skinny little
bitch, that young me, you kissed back then
how I won't let you come see me
how I'm thinking you might come marry me
if you ever get diabetic and go blind

Dove

Two weeks dying (longer, if I had truly listened, heard
your song diminish to gone when I returned
one day to home.) And then you could not fly
even as high as your one good wing had carried you,
to your water, to your seed. I saw you tip up your beak
to swallow water, to wet your long silent throat.
In the last days you huddled completely into an oval,
that shape we know as dove, smooth curve so like
Aladdin's lamp. I brought you tempting foods,
a peanut, buttered popcorn, suet, but you stumbled, you lay
on your back like the cartoon birds with X-ed out eyes,
and though I righted you, two times, three times, perhaps
it was a dozen, I who had not touched you in seven years,
in the last night you breathed like a man in a quiet sleep,
like someone I loved, breath steady beside me,
then the breath was a flicker, then the light went out
in your golden eyes. I took you in my hands, whole,
and surprisingly heavy, your hollow boned husk,
wrapped you in soft cloth, settled you into a mat
of dry grass.

In those last hours, I saw you pull into yourself, your light
gone to the heat of embers, the dear life crumbling
into that intense heat—and I saw how life goes on, how it chooses
to burn until nothing is wasted, almost nothing. What is
your soul but the blessing of stillness, silence? World,
dear living world, life that wishes to live—what flew
at last? You were teaching me to live. Let even my ash be of
use.

Downhill

we each drew a poster
to show the water cycle
from cloud to drop
to puddle brook
river lake
sea
and it seemed
that was the way
our lives would also go
needing always
a darker and
darker
blue

Dry Fly

Grandfather, this feather that I keep on my windowsill
I saved for you, grey, fraying, white at the edges,
saved for your hands to touch and shape,
new, as your life flown
forever into weightlessness, change, loss, hope.
Why did I never touch your hair?
I never said goodbye.

Durer–Study for Feet of a Kneeling Apostle

Not the steepled hands, but the soles of the feet,
bared and creased, folded, too soft to have borne
weight–imagine the ache, the hurt of arch against stone;
imagine the eagerness to rise, to be on about
the earth, but the rest in feet offered to air, the blessing
of the most vulnerable, least loved, most easily
forgotten sole, incapable of any expression but to yield.

Dusk

fragrance of pinecones
spilled beneath the waterfall
on darkening stones

one swallow alone
flies above the evening squall
fragrance of pinecones

a colder wind moans
late hawk and whippoorwill call
on darkening stones

like clattering bones
dry branches of winter, small
fragrance of pinecones

yet still late moon shone
against the cold mountain wall
fragrance of pinecones
on darkening stone

8/8/02

Today your grandson skipped a stone
one hop less than his years. You would
have been proud. Fifteen, he remembered
a day ten years ago on a little beach beside
the Wissahickon and how his older sister
caught on quick and we doubted that his little
hands could do it–but they did–skipped stones
then with your hands around them and today
it was fourteen skips and the sun was setting.
We watched crawdads in the shallows, bats
and swallows skimming low across the pond.
The rowboats rocked against their chains
but none of them was our boat, our boat
so many years, these forty years, gone

Enter Herman Mudgett

I had thought about buying the house in Franklin.
I like a house with a wrap-around porch.
Even enclosed, good for storage. Near
the road. And it had a center chimney. But
the copy said—'childhood home of notorious
Mudgett.' I figured I ought to find out who
that was. And I gotta admit I was kinda proud
to find out that the third most murderous
mass-murderer of all time grew up in my home
town, the man who built a Castle of Horrors
for the Chicago World Columbian Exposition—
no amusement ride, it was outwardly A Grand
Hotel, but within hid secret doors and chutes
to torture chambers and a crematorium in
the basement. Unbelievable but Real. All those
poor Irish maids and farmgirls boiled to lard
and sold as anatomic skeletons by one-time
medical student, now the resourceful (AKA)
Dr. Harry Holmes. Tried, hanged and buried
under ten feet of cement. So he wouldn't rise
again. I wonder who actually did buy the place.

Every poem I write for my father is called twilight

Clouds make shadows on the mountains.
I walk through their green darkness. I want
a wind to silence thought, a storm to drown
out prayer, electric stillness, the promise
of breaking. You can walk three days
into woods and not find a single birch

worth a canoe. I know. I have done it.
I have loved slender saplings peeled white
and mourned for their cracking death
in ice. You never trusted your canvas
to my hands, never taught me the courage

of rapids. But I learned to read cocoons
and the wings of beetles, spider silk
and the veins of fern. I can follow bear
spoor studded with blackberry seed,
walk through thorns and not care if my legs

are bloodied. I have knelt on bruised knees,
mouth to rough water, asked the snake
to rattle your path from his one rock.
I want to remember dawn. I will listen for
the hawk to fold his wings.

Fall Lambs

I pulled over to look at fall leaves and to talk to you,
the most serious of conversations, and then my words
were choked off, swallowed, as a bright red flag
unfurled from the rump of a ewe, became a purple gush,
saw her quick licking of the heavy lump and its
staggering rise to pink-eared whiteness, a miracle,
and even more—I had not expected, the other dropped,
and the mother, perhaps too tired to turn to more work,
or too in love with one newborn, the twin lay still,
ignored, until a child came from the shepherd's house, lifted
the first lamb in her arms, carried it away, and the mother bent
to that second bundle and began her heavy kiss

Final

Walking through the old house for the last time
you have begun to vanish. The once gold
carpeting is lumped and faded. There,
the path beneath the blanket chest is bold
and new, a shock against thirty years;
and the windows are streaked, fine
cobwebs where you thought them clean,
that spinning dust, those little dancers
in the space of sunlight through each open
door. You shut them, one by once, no answer
from the empty rooms, then search again
each closet but there's nothing gleaned
Pause a moment by the backstairs, see,
the house is empty, door locked, you have no key

Forbidden Drive

I choose to look upstream.
Trees have straggled and grown
from the dust collected in the scars
of the stone bridge.

Upstream, against the gray stone sky,
are colors: copper, bronze, gold.
Water sounds, peepers, faraway traffic.

Downstream must be just as beautiful
but I am anxious watching water
flow away.

Rust.

Three yellow leaves
fall together;
are becalmed
in silt and rock.

I turn to face
the coming water
before they are carried
away.

Forest service

When we were children
we collected fall leaves;

we gathered hundreds,
many colors;

we coated them with wax,
pressed between the pages of a book;

we ordered them by size, shape
species, color, age;

we climbed trees,
reached out to the end of branches,

took leaves from tiny trees
along forgotten logging roads;

we scraped away ice,
crawled over frozen waterfalls:

there was no perfect leaf
they were all dying.

Forsaking

I called them bluets and perhaps they were:
blossoms as small as a child's fingernail,
four tiny white petals threaded with blue
each slender stem thinner than baby hair.
I plucked them and bunched them in one dirty
fist, then saw the red, red strawberry, wild,
small as a prayer bead. I picked one, tasted,
sweet, flowers stuffed in my pocket, plucked more,
one more, another, filled the next pocket
sat with stained lips and fingers, saw the long
way back.

Foundation

Someone built a farm here, someone came
in early spring with hope and empty hands—
not a scrap is left, not even his name.

Summer brought no rain. His fields became
brown, withered, dust from once rich land.
Someone built a farm here, someone came

with a hungry family, without blame
fell further into poverty. To this man
not a scrap is left, not even his name

is saved. His gaunt face fading, always the same
grim sepia portraits, understand :
someone built a farm here, someone came

to harvest only stones, to harvest shame,
to fail to feed his family, scattered like sand.
Not a scrap is left, not even his name.

The house has sunken, its walls could not withstand
years of emptiness, left to reprimand:
someone built a farm here, someone came.
Not a scrap is left, not even his name.

Friend Cow

contemplating the prayer of her cud
abundant cathedral of oats and oat dust
rising, spiraling, light fading heights
this silo a steeple
this stall a tomb
of green flies trapped against never washed windows
I bow to you face against
your great sturdy haunches
pink udder, pink nose
long-lashed eyes filled with mine

Gathered Meeting

The lame meet the sick.
Some of us wear our deformities
Every day. Some come together.
Some are alone. I envy the families.
You recognize the brothers and sisters
who have sat through four generations,
the spouses now grown to closer resemblance
than kin. Some sat in this room eight decades ago.
Perhaps that one stuck his stocking feet on the bench
back just like those purple toes poking in front of me;
yes, that one with the thin white hair was calmed
by holding her father's gold watch. Children.
Babies. I think of a poem where the poet
began to picture everyone as a baby.
I try it. Now there is a meditation.
Is it the potential or the weakness,
the miracle or the need? Look
at each one, imagine, then
see this, not just at birth
but at eight or eighteen
or eighty, still there,
the possibility, the vulnerability,
fierceness, the beauty, the open mouth,
the open hand, selfishness, selflessness, godspeed.

The Gilford Community Band Concert

July 15, 1998
—*our twenty-first season*–

All rise for
THE STAR-SPANGLED BANNER

>My mother was against it.
>Five thousand dollar bicentennial grant
>used to build a bandstand
>on the village field.
>Better spent: books for the library.
>She and Polly, two middle-aged library aides, considered
>graffiti, shook cans of red spray paint:
>"This Bicentennial Gazebo Sucks."

(now the band has overflowed the stand;
the percussionists stand under an awning off the back.)

I throw a worn quilt down for the children.
THE WASHINGTON GRAYS MARCH

>The heads around me are white–
>white as my father's; I search for him
>in the crowd. I recognize no one,
>no face, his generation (or mine.)

Feet move, canes rap.
IN THE MOOD

Mother's dance a twisting dance
holding their babies' hands.
A stooped woman takes a toddler's hand,
twirl and laugh, twirl and laugh.
There are more couples here,
more old men than one might expect.

Light changes, gold.
THE BELLE OF THE BALL

A young girl, hair the color
of an Irish setter, falling to her waist,
skin the color of skim milk,
steps away with a black and white dog
and a boy whose head just reaches her shoulder.

They go the edge of the field to smoke.
She returns with a small bouquet
of wildflowers, curtsies,
presents them to a woman with
a copper bowl of hair.

Coughs, paper flutter.
PUTTIN' ON THE RITZ

A man runs, pulling a small daughter by the hand.
A toddler runs, laughing, ahead.
Scurry, scurry, scoot.
Scoop up a laugh.

Salmon sky–blue and pink–no moments unchanged.
PAVANNE

Sun falls through branches beside the brook.
Clouds light, flicker, wait for stars.
White birch limbs, bared by last year's ice
frame the steeple beyond the field.

Up, up, up, teach the children to lift their knees.
BARNUM & BAILEY'S FAVORITE MARCH

    Girls do bent-leg cartwheels behind the drums.
    A gold puppy, arriving late, pulls
    his children around the bandstand
    in the quick-step parade.

    "It'll cool off, sure,
    and then the bugs'll come out."

INTERMISSION

    "Try this, it works pretty good,
    put some on your ankles, there, wrist, neck."

The field hockey teams arrives clattering.
THE CHILDREN OF THE REGIMENT

    Hockey sticks and tennis rackets,
    boys with coke and chips.
    Chairs fill for a moment,
    then all race to run and climb

    on each other's backs in the
    the settling light.

Stillness, distant voices.
IT'S THE GOSPEL

>The girl with milk white hands
>presses a bundle of ferns
>and daisies into the hands
>of the grandmother
>enthroned.

Dark, chill.
UNDER THE BOARDWALK

>Children bundle down,
>thumbs and blankets,
>blue-black sky.

>Wind, flickers, crying, gone.
CRIMEBUSTERS

>Alan, who is 38 and cannot read,
>waits by his bike to give a program
>to any last stragglers in.

A hand clasps my shoulder
THE BATTLE HYMN OF THE REPUBLIC

>Welcome home.

>The children begin the circling lope around the bandstand.

–fine–

>March, run, march, clap in rhythm, clap.

ENCORE
Stand, clap, march, run.
THE STARS AND STRIPES FOREVER
    Struggle, fold blanket, chairs, gather cups;
    little street a moment busy;
    let the too friendly cat out of
    the barn.

Golden child, Wood, Ash

In those days children could wander
alone in the woods. We trusted trees.
We even trusted people. The stranger
with candy sounded like myth, like
the witch in the Black Forrest, the Ice
Queen, Blue Beard, Lucifer. A child
of five could wander all day in a meadow
picking flowers, could pack her lunch
in a paper bag and drink Kool
Aid out of a thermos, share
an apple with ants. Her mother
could sit all day over coffee and breaking
marriages with the other mothers. People
went into each other's houses through
unlocked doors. TV didn't play
until evenings, radios played only
sad songs. The children listened.
On lost dirt roads and along fading rivers
they the sang 'on the wings
of a snow white dove' and 'Johnny
don't leave me. Johnny be true.'
Sang those other songs too, songs
that were only rhythm and sobbing.
Songs of the birds they were, whose wings
were breaking as they entered the world
nobody'd expected.

Hair Wreath, 1865

—with thanks to Don LaBranche

I have let go my braids. Let there be locks
of the living bound with those of the dead—
yours come coiled, wound tight in the broken watch
the boy carried six months from Shiloh, red
bright as all the Thomases, your brother's,
our son's, (now a dozen rosebuds twisted
with the gray I make into leaves—mother's
nearly white now, thinning.) I have let go
my braids. They will grow back for another
spring's lambing—or fall—your curls made a rose
with mine, mouse brown, dusty brown, dutiful
brown, easily forgotten, that I wove
with yours once, in our meadow, bountiful
my braids, undone, your whisper, beautiful

Hiroshima Day

I had forgotten how long a trip it was:
a rush past swamps, then turn at the Bear Camp River:
follow it, look for the cabin that might be Anna's . . .
Things quiet; trees shuffle, form a covered bridge—
we nearly miss its cool darkness—
Then the road is dirt and climbing.
Late, I swerve into the field to park.
I've always meant to make this day special to the children.
We should fold paper boats and float candles on the brook
at sunset, remembering, pondering, hallowing . . .

A snake lies backbroken and belly flat—the frog in its mouth
fights but cannot outlive the dying snakejaw. I step across
to take the children's hands. Life, I say, it is life, it is part of life.
I pull children and push lingering adults up the hill,
eight orthodox Philadelphia Quakers attending
a Hicksite meeting in North Sandwich, NH.
The last to turn, the scientist, takes
a stick and flings the leavings
toward the piled up stones along the road.

Home Burial

–for A.W.

It wasn't done anymore
yet he wished it, so we laid
the body out on the dining room table,
the room unused since Myrtle's death,
pulled the shade, and each neighbor
came to sit a quarter hour in the chair
at its feet. As always, women
left pies on the kitchen counter, pots
of soup to warm for Paul on the stove,
a pitcher of iced coffee set
in the 'fridge; and on the morning
of the third day Paul hitched the tractor
to the flatbed, secured the coffin
with thick rope and chains, steadied
the brakes for the trip down
the long hill. People paused in their
driveways. Some put a hand
over their hearts as if his father
were the flag, his passing a sign:
at eighty-three, we thought him
the last farmer in town, yet
they found a dozen others to carry
him to his place at Myrtle's side.

Honest things

—for John

my neighbors '74 pickup, red body, blue hood,
rakes and shovels tied to the side with electric
cords; the fence made of painted doors; white
washed tires cut into scalloped planters; blessed
Mary protected by an upturned bathtub; that sunken
barn in a scarred field; fishline and a pair of bobbers
caught in poplar branches; your rowboat; your rawhide
laces tied three times around your ankle; the mudcaked
boots on the smoothed doorstep; the garage window
patched with cardboard; the flag pole used
as a tomato stake; the 1963 license plate from
your brother's 1957 Harley; that cracked
leather jacket; your scarred fingernail; the scar
across the palm of your hand; my real bowie knife
with chipped bone handle; your hammer, the one
I painted red; shower curtains used as drop clothes;
clotheslines; clothespins; your hat, the one you didn't take.

Hoyt Road

Come to the little brook with me, I'll show
you dappled things and fish that greenling go
and pollywogs in jelly and the spit
a spit bug makes on grasses sheltering it,
I'll tell you that it's snake spit and you'll run
away down meadows shining in the sun
and when I pin your hands behind your back
I'll kiss you then until you kiss me back.

I am watching the sparrow

honoring each day
as it sinks into earth
dear brown, shadowed
by stillness, ridge,
feathers darkening
to hard black nib
wings become fallen
leaves, bones a basket
holding dust. I do not
touch this memorial.
No voice blessing
or mourning. Fall is
falling on my heart.

I cannot say how deep the snow

but sometimes it piled deep as a man
can stand and the children made a run
from the pinewood to the great banks

at the road—we mothers stood
as if we could slow their speed,
catch disaster at a passing car,

our furred feet trudging, breaking
the crust that held their lighter
bodies. Icicles that could kill

hung two stories long, pulled eaves
in sighing creaks—snow seeped
along the window sills, sneaked

into the bedrooms on the second
floor. Fires steamed
in every room. Our clothes layered,

movements muffled, we were
stumbling bears, walking tree
stumps. Then, surprised,

in the white field that had been
our garden, we catch a glimpse of blue
lift and show the children, crisp

in our mittened hand
a shard emerging
sprung from another time,

blue-veined, ivory, ancient
willow china, once cast away, broken,
beautiful now as cold gives it release

Improvements

They tried to improve the Village
Store. The deli counter failed; so did
the cut-out window for ice cream
and the big old addition in the garage
for local arts and crafts turned out
to be not worth heating. The home
made bread went stale in baskets
on the porch, the cordwood never
moved, the local corn wilted, even
the live bait concession died out. What
sells–gas, two pumps out front, pump
first, pull away before you pay, coffee
to go near the register, cigarettes, and
six packs and cases of beer.

In the City of Widows the One Old Man is King

he has a dozen sweethearts
they save a seat for him
at the luncheon table
buy him special biscuits
knit hats and scarves and mittens
sing a breaking harmony
to his war songs and laments
they do not touch him
but they keep their eyes
turned toward him
they do not touch him
but they would like
a reason to take his hand

It was perhaps thirty-five years ago

the summer the scarlet tanagers came
out of the woods to die. I had glimpsed one
once or twice in deep woods but now saw glow
that sad bright red paint-splattered blacktop, pain
everywhere, feathers pressed and waving slowly
from hot tar. I do not know what caused it,
the exodus, perhaps a disturbance
in weather, a destruction of forest,
a change in the food supply, and they'd rest
their bodies in the sun to die; but what death,
beauty, and what more beauty beyond the reach
of our slow and limited creature sight
waits until our vision be stunned into light?

Lit

I wanted
to be
a clear
cold stream:
that you
might drink
and be
refreshed

The Jar

Oh, and it was a fine thing to go with my father
in early spring to the sporting goods store at Paugus Bay,
just the beginning of the season for landlocked salmon and
the big lake itself unlocking. A few pickups pointed
at forgotten roadblocks in the withered grey snowbanks.
Inside: the taxidermy, great fierce heads, bear and
puma, mountain goat and bison; even the small
beasts turned to snarl, teeth bared, raccoon and fox and fisher
cat—meanest animal known—boys said they left just the
skeleton of your family pet—but you could recognize it
by the collar still looped around the bones—and smart too,
the fisher, clever and sneaky, only animal could eat
a porcupine, circling round and around til it flopped dizzy
on its back and had its belly torn to shreds. Oh, the fisher,
rarely seen, but even squirrels were fierce, and beaver and skunk
and owl and bat, ruffled grouse and wolverine, stalking dust
motes on shelves near the dimly lit ceiling; ah, but bright,
at my eye's level, the glass cases, packed with bullets and lead
weights and red and white bobbers and trout flies on a rack
that I could spin with a finger, dry flies and streamers,
grey ghost and mickey finn, and how many times had I watched
my father in dawn or sunset light spilt open the stomach
of the first trout, caught to read its contents, and choose
the best fly off his hat. I could tie a mickey finn at five,
red and yellow feathers, head a tight bead of black thread
and I learned to read from the labels in the trout fly book .
I could read, yes, and I waited always for the last queasy treat,
there just above my eye's level, at the cash register,
the great jar, its contents slowly bobbing, filmed blue black eyes

seen through white flesh, fetal limbs begging before each chest,
knees locked beneath the supplicant hooves, bobbing
in the fine white flakes of what would have been their skin,
eternal flurries dancing, the twin deer fetusses and the faded
brown label:
unborn, cut from a 75 pound doe, alive, winter, 1956.

Jee

Once upon a time I found a baby bird:
a small perfect robin, just feathered,
rust chest, short gray tail. Every hour
it asked to eat, beak open, bright yellow,
peep squeak peep. I fed it dry cat food
soaked in egg and milk. It grew. It followed
me around the dining room on hopping
twig legs. It slept in your room, quiet 'til
dawn and new hunger. One day we had
to go away, some business of your father's.
I set him carefully on the hay in the old
pony shed. When we came back the shed
was empty. And I saw there was a hole
beneath one wall big enough for a cat
to crawl or certainly one small bird to
fly. And it had just begun to fly. Small
hopping flights around the garden when
I took it out to watch me weed. I had
hoped to see it catch a worm, to know
it would survive when we set it free.
Free. We watched the sky for a week.
A month. I watch the sky now. Come
home. Come. We worry so. You are so
alone. I am so alone without you.

Jelly Bean, three

Annie Oakley rides the darkness
that slants through crib bars
to stripe the oak
floor and I love Spin
and Marty and sing a cowboy
song red hat hung
by the chinrope
on a duckbill coatrack home
I lead three Appaloosa mares
and a pair of buffalo
trusty wolf pack at
my heals
call sweet slow
rock rock dusty road
past moon and treetop wind
and someday I will know I know
the moment when I pass
to sleep

Johnson's

there was supposed to be a mule
to preside in the forward stall
beams hung with brass and leather, dusty ribbons
that silence in which animals move, that power
and I am a child

the cows stay as they are useful
the horse leaves his great collar behind
as he goes to slaughter
I have forgotten his name
the dappled white horse in the orchard

June

knows where to sit everybody–Pap and Mary
have to be at the booths with the ashtrays
and Ginny likes the table in the corner but
doesn't talk to her daughter Jean or that biker
she married even if the marriage has lasted
since 1973. Jean and Marie don't speak
although their husbands used to work together
at the ball bearing plant but Jean is usually
finished her lunch by the time Marie arrives
except on Tuesdays when she shops for her
mother first and is in later. Jean also doesn't
speak to her daughter Gina but does speak
to the granddaughter Jill if Gina leaves
the table. Gina's ex-husband Tom takes care
of Jean's car if it needs work. His second wife
Linda lost a baby last year so Jean helps them
spend some extra time with Jill. Mary used to
work with Marie before they closed the
bottling plant but Marie is reach touchy about
smoking since her Carl died so they never sit
together. Marie and Ginny used to go to catechism
together at St. Helena's but you'd never guess
they were the same age, Ginny never bothers
with her hair or make up. Looks about as old
as Pap and he's her father or is it stepfather
since he never married Mary. That about makes
him Jill's great great grandfather but he wouldn't
know it, he does like her red stick-out braids.)

Junior's Favorite Chocolate Cake

we thought women did nothing

they didn't work like fathers did

a coconut cake with white snowflake icing
wasn't work, nor hot-crossed buns
with drizzled sugar and dry flower dusting
nor a roast basted in the oven
six hours, lemon meringue pie,
three other desserts

my mother squeezed fresh orange juice
for my father each morning
while he was lying in bed

he had work to do
she had nothing

all day to clean house
his mother's tea waiting
in a thin china cup

Just now, in the new millennium, someone has discovered

that "squaw" was a Native American word,
(in some languages at least,) for the female genitalia,
hence it may also have been used to mean, "prostitute."
Town councils across New England, alerted to
this error, have recommended that the names
of an extremely large number of streets, lakes,
mountains, valleys, housing developments, shopping
malls, islands, streams, rivers, ponds, hills, etc., be changed
to what struck them at hand as an eminently
acceptable substitution: "Moose."

Kneading

When you were little there would sometimes come a snow
day and we would have the time to make bread,
mix great bowls of dough, cover with towels
by the radiator while we raced outside and built snowwomen
and forts and made snowballs to freeze until next summer,
then knead together and punch and fold and go out
and catch snowflakes on dark wool to test uniqueness
under glass and knead again, taste snow on our tongues
and steam wet mittens on the radiator while bread baked
and I was the best mother in the world because I was home
and given time I never expected it all to be taken away;
I have never baked bread alone

Landscape

Do I hold the shape of the lake in my mind
spilled out into forests below the black hills?
Could I blindfolded trace its bays and its inlets,
the Broads and the channels, harbors and isles?
Will I only make blueness, cut into green fabric,
empty, unreal, unguided; untrue as the light I
imagine now kisses my eyelids as hillside I rest
before lifting the sweetness of blueberries up
to my lips?

The last thing my father told me:

If you go down
to the basement
and stand
with your back
against my work bench
you'll see a long wooden box up in the beams.
You might remember it.
I made it forty years ago.
It contains two bamboo Orvis fly rods.
The older one is worth at least a thousand dollars.
There's plenty of people would want to buy them.
Orvis doesn't sell them any longer.
The guys who knew how to make them
have all died out.
There won't be any more.

Limit

He has been caught in a squall
that raises like angry men the trees
around the river and whips his hair
into a hollowed bank. Man that he is
he makes use of the time–while darkness
signals a neverending flood he counts flies–
248 on a hat band–726 on a vest–1320
in clasped metal envelopes folded in
a pocket. The storm lifts. He builds
a fire. He redoes the count while his
clothes dry. Goes home with his limit.

Lit

Late afternoon light
I row the great boat with long oars.
It circles to my uneven pull,
til ten trout swim
in dark water
in the wire box hooked
on the stern.
Sun glare
Ice trees light the frozen cascade to the lake.
Lashes locked by frozen tears
I tuck and race my father
to the bottom of the trail.

Butter fog
Sunday morning, drizzled mist on creaking mud,
we kneel beside the lake's cathedral
ice;

Dim white bulb dust
Feet hooked into the bars of the stool
I block my ears. My father,
bit tongue and steady hands,
slides a board against the saw.

White
Noon climb hot,
skin sizzling bug lowland to leaf green gold height:
May, October seek
one pine standing alone

Womb dark
Canoe dip and drip.
Oars lay on gunwales,
balance, tense,
listen: loon.

Lumber

You held me to the skies:
pale spring, deep blue summer,
autumnal burn, winter nights
and sharp still stars. I lay unafraid
in your arms. I was a part of all
you were: strength, tenacity,
abundance, shelter, home.
You shielded me, invisible,
suspended in air, lifted by wind;
my reluctant feet dropped to
the stones when human voices
called. I thought you would live
forever, that my children would
know you, bless you as I blessed
you. Young myself, I went away.
You were alone when they cut
you, tore out your roots: more
room for the cemetery. May
mourners hear your acorns
sing to life upon the rocks.

Marvel

that a blue bell
becomes a berry
and a berry
becomes a bear

and they both clothe
the mountain
and feed the sweet
soft dirt

Mastery

My father decided to learn
to make baskets. He went
to craft fairs to compare
the various artists' work.
After a few years he decided
that he had the most respect
for a young craftswoman
who lived in a neighboring
county. He drove out to her
place and found her in her
garden. She took him with her
to a nearby marsh. They gathered
armsfull of reeds and set them
to soak. He came back the next
week. They built frames and began
the work of bending. She explained
a variety of weaves. He choose
a simple pattern. He worked
under her silent eye. He made
only one basket. Completed in
his seventieth year. He gave
it to me. He fulfilled
his commitment and moved on.

Matins

I have needed to lay my skin
on a sunwarmed stone. Even my palm
has not touched rock, my face feels only sad
air and dim autumn light waking and passing
the harsh electric rooms of probe and exam.
I touch no green with anything but my teeth;
only filth passes my fingers and a tissue
of false protection. A child, I lay under skies
that grew to the hem of eagles and heard grass
singing wisdoms my grandmothers had forgotten.
I knew the taste of clover and wild strawberry
and the scent of the flower that lives
in the shaded shallows of the brook. I knew
the embrace of the arched tree and the bed
the deer made beneath pines in the snow.
I read the color of light in ice caves
under lake and on the belly of a living
fish. I sang. I sang. Knowing no one
heard. These days fleeter than two hours
bent over form and protocol under my heavy
head, these eyes which never wake to starsong
darkmusic or a bird at midnight.

Meeting for Worship

Waiting in the silence
your breath brushed cool against my forearm
as you leaned to put your head
into your hands.

I thought:
always and whatever happens
this breath will be a part
of whatever breeze
cools me.

All was blessed.
I could not imagine a time
for myself or any other
creature: animal, plant, insect, bird,
that was not full of this beauty
or would ever again
be pain.

Melba may be 103

but my mother says it's not fair
to give her the Boston Post Cane
because even if she was a life-long resident
and her family goes back
two hundred years in the village
her nursing home's over
the county line and the cane is for
the oldest   r e s i d e n t so
just because her family
donated a lot of money
to the hospital and gave the land
for the Potter Home she doesn't
deserves special privileges
and Buddy's coming up on 102
and he only went to the Home
at 99 so he lived in town longer than
she did, leaving when she was widowed
at 93. I say Mother, quit fussing
that cane's the kiss of death, just like
being the Grand Marshall
in the Old Home Day parade.
You know somebody's coming up
on you, eying that gold-plated
handle, 101, 102, girl
better watch her back.

Milo at the Bandstand

Joined the Grange when I was seventeen,
1937, same year as Bertha Hoyt,
she was a few years older than me, taught
at that school forty and more years. You'd a thought
some one of her students would have come
to the funeral. I spoke to Rob Varney,
guess he had something else to do.
My grandfather came here to preach
in 1902. Married my parents
right in that house there,
used to be the Methodist parsonage,
that's how I came to be born here,
lived all my life here—so far—that's eighty years.
Your mother tell you I called on her? Thought she
might have mentioned it. Might call on her again.
My Sally's been dead twelve years now.
Good to have a meal with someone. Just got
eight chickens now, all hens, get about six eggs
on a good week, they're not young 'uns; six head
of cattle, most the fields' just hay. Keep a good
garden though. Might bring a little something down
to your mother's. What you think she might like?
Blueberries? Does she like to make a pie?
Lemon meringue? I'll save up some eggs.

Morning

Woke up this morning

And the first sun bronzed down on the puddles
(they were carnival glass; twisted
crinkling gold and red, purpling
in sea shell edges against the
black, and shining darkly, smooth
and rippled, reflecting, strengthening
the sun)

And the clouds framed, then hid the sun
(they were end-of-the-day; pink, shot
through with the colors of the day—
before red, blue, green and gold–
with this day the colors merged
to lazy dove's ear pink in the light
slanting through)

And the sun hung over the mountain
(it was a cranberry jewel; purple
and red, angry, rising higher
with shades of gold mixed in black,
black, roundly perfect, sharply
cut ember-jewel faceted by the
passing clouds)

And I wanted to say "look at the sky"
(it will never again be that day,
the fragile glass all shattered

with noon or froze in quiet
color, shining dull, the broken
pieces can never be glued again
into that sky)

But I couldn't say it
And it rained

The Murderer of Crows

Last night a flight of crows passed overhead,
each larger than the last with louder squawks,
and shrieking mobbing anger filled the woods—
this morning bloody talons mark the snow;

I've watched the owlets choke down prey alive
when they were hardly cracked out of the egg:
songbird, muskrat, squirrel, and once a snake
twisting, writhing, as if it could still strike—

we might yet see the owl but not her prey,
it lies a pile of feathers with the bones
gulped whole and spat out eyeless with the beak,
fragments of skull, rib, wishbone, but the feet,

one of the dead crow's feet, is missing:
and there's the owl, she's flopping like an old
woman leading off the fancy dancing,
her wide tail shakes, a feather fan held blessing

the sacred drum, her wings curved like a
beaded shawl. Her foot stamps mark that steady
tremor: I see it now, the dead crow's foot
is tightly clamped onto the grounded owl's

left talon. She's crippled. Caught up in roots
and creeping vine and mud, in terror, mad
for flight yet tangled tightly bound to earth.
Will the creature she killed now kill her?

Night visitor

your hands, lovely silver, in the pockets
of night—I was a girl turned shaman, daughter
of beasts, shadow, part of the moon, little
goddess, companion, speaking wordless
to creatures who delicate, took stale
bread and mold-brushed grapes
from my hands, I knew bliss as you stepped
less and less far from my whispers with each scrap,
and stayed at last within the circle of reflected
firelight, your masked eyes wise, whiskers
sensitive, your friendship a gift
for a lonely child, your sweet stripes
trusting my hands—you came wild and real
into my presence, this was power, transformation—
you made me wild, you made me real

Nursing

see your mother nod
she twists a cold rosary
for the love of God

heavy with regard
you braid her last vanity
see your mother nod

she gives you words to guard
broken, brittle memory
for the love of God

listen to the words
she says it is your legacy
see your mother nod

what is it you laud?
is it your own frailty?
for the love of God

frail divining rods
tapping out an elegy
see your mother nod
for the love of God

Off Nantucket

Honor:

That all parts of the whale are useful
That ambergris, bile and vomit of whales, makes exquisite
fragrance
That blubber nourishes in arctic cold and whale meat is a good
source of protein, valued
    in famine
That the skin of the whale contains Vitamin C

Praise:

That whale-bone cinched the waists of faint Victorian women
and bowed out their
hooped skirts
That whale oil burns slow and clean
That cetyl alcohol is a useful as lubricant and emollient and
spermaceti for ointments and
    candles

Respect:

That whale teeth and bone and baleen and the tusks of walrus
become scrimshaw in
    hands with lonely hours and the polished tabua is a gift to one
of great esteem
That baleen was made into buggy-whips and parasol ribs and into
smooth tools to crease
    paper in the making of fine books

Rejoice:

That the whale is beautiful
That it may migrate 10,000 miles in a single year
That it nurses its young on rich and fatty milk
That it approaches boats with friendly curiosity
That its cousin dolphins fish cooperatively with men in Myanmar and Brazil

Lament:

That at least ten species of whales are endangered
That stone-age man hunted whales by skin-boat spear
That we sail against the whale now with metal factory ships
That harpoons explode within the whale's body
That a whale was found with a 125 year old New Bedford harpoon fragment embedded in
    its side

Exult:

That the Nantucket sleighride has ceased, that thing of sublime power and fear
That now only one wooden boat from the 'heyday' of whaling remains berthed at Mystic

In Glory:

That the song of the whale is beautiful
That its tears protect its eyes from the sting of salt

The Pest House

It was the place I went to as a child
alone: an abandoned farmhouse a mile
or so from the village. They carried
the sick there. Those still strongest cared
for the weak, bathed them, dressed them
laid them out; buried the dead in a widow's
forgotten patch of violets behind
the kitchen door. All would die.
The village doctor left his horse
on the other side of the brook where
Lincoln Talbot drowned; he called in
instructions from the road.

When they saw the fire the villagers
brought buckets. They filled them
with water but seeing what burned
stood with heavy hands. They never
crossed. They watched it flame out
then walked back to their own fires.
It is said that five brothers had been among
the strong. That they were trapped
in the cellar when the house caved in.

Five pine trees grew from the ashes.
Grew fast. Grew large. Grew strong
One at each corner of the cellar hole's
great stones and the greatest overarching
the chimneypiece.

This was a sacred place. When a sixth tree
grew it was lightning struck: again,
the villagers saw fire. There was no need
to fight it. This time the brothers did not burn.
They let me come though. Let me wrap
child arms in greeting turning, walking,
around each trunk. Let me pry bricks from
the dooryard but never a bone. I wanted
to show my children. But it is gone.
Brought bad luck upon a new two story split level.
Just a plaque on a stone beside the road:
Here, in the yellow fever epidemic of 1793. . . .

Piper

where the mountain gleamed to stoneface
they old built greatrock thrones

that we might sit Gods a moment
over lichen and scrub oak
spruce and wind bent birch
and beyond the forest ridge

our little town shining
in white perfect calm

Presidentials

Here were mountains, tumbled, hard,
one great stone cleaved by an axe
of wind, ice, and the unforgiving cold.
Men meant nothing: shouts lost
in torrents, caught by crevasses, crack
of fallen rock. Yet there is a road,
a black thread on which these small men
crawled and cut their silent way
into the heart of stone, followed
the notch cut by the river, rode
that snake into the north, raised fire
with brittle muscle, found their way
into solitude, became bone on the edge
of the echoing ravine.

Ray at Town Hall knows a lot about payphones.

Before he was a deputy sheriff he was security
manager for all the payphones in all Northern
New England. There were 15,000 payphones
in Maine, New Hampshire and Vermont in 1992.
They were a major source of income for the phone
companies. Each coin box could hold $200.
Collections were taken daily by armored cars
to Boston. It was good business before cell phones.
Ray has a payphone at his home. He was given
a chrome-plated one by the company on retirement.
He says it's hooked up and his grandchildren
'get a real kick' out of using it. However, it is not
the last payphone in Gilford. The last one is
in the main lodge at Gunstock ski area just across
from the Powder Keg. Bill, in Sales and Marketing,
says 'Maybe we'll use it in an advertising brochure.'

Reincarnation

Better I see you as a hummingbird
with a love for color and fragrance, and I
your tiny mother, sweet fanning your
gentle egg; better you as the lily that we
danced to in late July, I the arching stalk
to bear the blossom you have been, better
you remembered as the skink darting
dark cool tunneling shadows, I your quick-
tailed mother in search of a quiet nest;
the hedgehog child and her bristling parent
slow-crossing a too loud highway, an ant
returning with breadcrumbs to sweeten
her mother queen; better I be your fawnling,
and nuzzle your tender belly; better you be
father penguin, and rock me on bright red feet.

Remind me to take you

next time it's August and grasshoppers are snapping
in the tall grass and seabirds come ashore tap tap
for insects in the parched cemetery grass
there, behind Red Watson's place, down
cart tracks left a century ago
to the little pool left
below a broken bridge
under the arch of a fallen
log there where
it is cool

Right after I won second place for the state of New Hampshire in the Betty Crocker Search for the Homemaker of Tomorrow

A boy argued that the contest was unfair as it excluded males and so
the not-so-subtle change was made to "Family Leaders"; meanwhile
the Home Ec suite at Laconia High School, long fallen into disuse,
was one day disassembled. Gone the living room with ugly gray cut velvet couch, the dinette set, the half bed (as seen in furniture showrooms,) folded like a bad-perspective hallucination of itself. Gone
the kitchen with its sweet tie-back curtains overlooking the bricks of the industrial arts wing. Gone the copper bottom pots and tea cozy, bosom-ruffled aprons and silver tea set. I'd never learned there anyway. I barely cook. If I'd won first I'd a been found out at the bake off or the 'tea for senator's wives in our nation's capitol.'
For a few years I got the newsletter, read which state winners and
runner-ups had placed in the canning competition at which state fair
and I looked forward to them running the news of my graduation from medical school. I wanted to comment on the periodic interview
questions. I should have been more respectful. Now they call it Family Consumer Science and I have nearly consumed myself to death.

Rosary Hill

—for Jordan L. White, Sr.

It had been a slow dying. I overheard talk:
that the sisters would give all that was needed
at the end to stop pain. I never saw them. I
did not go to the funeral. I stayed at home with
visions of silent crows with white hands. But I
went with my father when he did this one last
thing–the un-wiring. My grandfather, his father
had been an inventor, unrecognized; a janitor,
a custodian, to others, his true life's work was
the system, the automation, of his building,
the great clockwork that fired the furnace, lit
the halls, rolled the heavy barrels of trash, tipped
ramps to the dumbwaiter, ignited its motors,
opened its doors, rang bells, buzzed, called,
two dozen households, fuses, lamps, speakers,
recorders, cameras, all in circuit. In my grandmother's
mind it must all malfunction and seize (I am told
she swore but once in her life–the day she returned
from visiting her sister and woke to a storm, to windows
slammed all around her by unseen hands; 'another
Bob White Gadget, what every household needs .')
I do not know what my father felt, clipping wires,
unplugging circuit boards. Only that the dying was
now more final, that she had made it complete.

The Sweetest Water in the World

I will find
the place
where the deer make
their beds
in the snow
and lie down.

Round Pond

Always twilight. I pull the heavy oars
through dark water until we balance,
cool air and water, night stilling, silent,
but for the living web of insect song spun
to our skin. We could hear a fly
settle on the face of the pond, hear the fish
rise to meet it, the still circles of each rise
ringing out until each fish's hunger met
our wooden boat and quavered back.

Night birds dipped, smooth swallows,
flickering bats; no human sound
but the shipped oars dripping and
the shirr, shirr, shirr as my father gathered
the line in his palm for the cast,
the quick run-out as the trout pulled taut,
the moonlit silver dulling in the dark creel.

My father knew each hatch, which mayflies
lived for only one night's flight, or two,
or three, or five. He knew the larva
and the nymphs, each swimming, clinging,
crawling stage. He'd catch a chrysalis
on the net's edge to watch the rough husk split
then dry and enter air. So many white wings.

He'd lean a moment, the lit match quick
against his young face, the cigarette cupped,
match shaken, his hands brisk to tie a leader

or untangle a knot. I wet a finger. No wind.
Moon. I lay on the bottom of the drifting
boat, rocking, palms open to stars, so many
risings, light, sound, circles, whispers of fish,
my father dim in the bow, casting and reeling in,
my whispering breath, the water gentling,
lapping, and he rowed us swiftly home.

The Society of the Second Coming of Christ Jesus on Earth

Ann Lee went with her husband, the butcher,
to silent meeting in the neighbor's house;
commonly those in power broke up the meetings,
one jailed, another beaten when he did not remove
his hat.

Ann Lee buried her children watched her body bleed,
wrested power to turn from her husband to stop his fists.

Ann Lee sailed to America danced in the fields
at Waterlievet; a Quaker now she shook with power
used her body to summon spirit.

Ann Lee returned to virgin, mother of no one
mother of all danced naked channeled spirits—
people buried in land she would fill with her bones.

Mother Ann the second coming female messiah
dances dances in darkness dances in mist
feet pounding grown to hundreds advancing
dancing in steady purpose mighty thousands
palms lifted across doubled floors.

(They draw pictures of their visions, roll them up,
put them away.)

Eldress Bertha and Eldress Gertrude orphan children
taken in educated sign the Covenant;

in another century sit together on a metal cart
feet swing bonnet strings dangle old women
with faces of children.

Dill, mint, apple, rosemary: five pies a day.

(Celibacy seems to imply long life or is it the energy
of dancing feet?)

Twelve women left in New England, an argument;
most decide to close the Covenant; the experiment is ended
the second coming closed.

(Forget the apostates at Sabbathday.)

Beside the hearth at Canterbury waits a cradle carved
for an adult: grandmother's cradle hold dimming body
after sight after hearing after taste after smell
body left with rhythm only rocking steady carried to
the third coming
home.

So Much to Learn About a Simple Fish

And I never did. I let silence sit
between us, and where the child
was content, or let her eager voice
spill, not requiring an answer, the grown
daughter believed she had to fill
pauses with meaning, pull concern.
But the pause was meaning, was
the lesson. I didn't hear.

I should have asked him about trout.
I could have learned. The awful numbers
life required, the need for joining
and death, the vigilance
to what would sustain. And beauty
in design, as the fish sees reflected
light and cannot see what lies precisely

before it. He studied, learned
what was needed. To step in a river
to his hips and know how to stand.
A life's work, to be perfect in this
one thing. A thing to be done alone.
That required silence. The seizure
of what is free. The letting go.

Stone House

—for Fred Outwater

I have gone to sleep in my grandfather's house.
It is not really any room, just beds loaded with lots
of quilts and blankets in the stair well and landing.

I sleep very soundly. Two women come to wake us.
I try to explain to them that I am Venie's granddaughter,
that I have come home. I want you to see every detail

of this house he made. The great stone porch. The
long living room with two doors opening to it. The
great stone fireplace. All stone. He loved stone.

And wood. The great polished wood on the banister.
There should be a Tiffany lamp in the dining room.
I want to show you where Edie sat, blind, rocking. I want

to take you to the barn in the back and show you the
tools the tools the tools. That is something I know
you can appreciate. The women are making up

all the beds. They are cooking on the big stove.
They are washing linens in the sink. They do not understand
who I am but they are telling me about their illnesses.

They let me stay. They show me their scars. We look
out the kitchen door. The family is gone. You are gone.
Women remain, working. We tuck ourselves in.
We learn each other's names.

Stripping

It's still icy run off
but the little crowd's gathered along the roadside's
in shirtsleeves
munching maple sugar-on-snow
and the white white glint of afternoon sun on snow
is dazzling as the quick silver
of salmon lifted
from the dying falls into the motionless canal

the men's bright gloved hands
squeeze-strip-slip milt into buckets
slosh and the fish is bumping
with a hundred others in a glass-
walled lock—

they are denied
the little brooks,
riverlets of their birth
no true spawning, no clean
nests of pushed pebbles

land-locked, they have a chance at renewal,
don't turn
the senile red of their beaked ocean cousins,
but I don't know if these captives
live past this emptying,
if men return
them to the lake
or if their dulling muscle goes

to dankly fertilize
cow corn or to waste

and what I remember as a festival
of spring must really come
with dying light in fall
but the little egg-lets
the fingerlings
glow in their haunted aquariae
months, years, then a handslength,
stock again
my heavy lake

Summer I Run through the Meadows and Count the Cow Pies

The milkman places two bottles in the metal box on the porch
    Warm summer mornings and winters of ice
My mother leans from the door in her bathrobe
Fills a cool pitcher to place on the table

The school bus waits as the cows go out to pasture in the morning
    They shake their heavy heads and little rope tails
The children lean from the windows to mock them
Mooing and swishing and chewing gum cud

I wait alone for the cows in the evening
    They trudge back to the barn slowly, the sun's going down
One balks for a moment at the barn's heavy doorway
The others strain their necks to see in

The milkman places two bottles in the metal box on the porch
    Warm summer mornings and winters of ice
My mother leans from the door in her bathrobe
Fills a cool pitcher to place on the table

Swallows

two swallows built their nest upon one shutter
of the kitchen window beside your door
you might think such a small thing wouldn't matter

but each day I'd pause to hear their babies chatter
for insects, watch the parents search for more
two swallows built their nest upon one shutter

when evening came the birds would swoop and flutter
their beauty filled the evening sky once more
you might think such a small thing wouldn't matter

but something in their movements was so tender
something moved this child at her still core
two swallows built their nest upon one shutter

swift silent wings against a day of clutter
brief moment of peace and hope that I could store
you might think such a small thing wouldn't matter

now just a few limp sticks lie in the gutter
in darkness, lonely, I remember more
two swallows built their nest upon one shutter
you might think such a small thing wouldn't matter

Sweet

Edie, blind and ninety-seven, strapped
to a white enameled bed in the Hudson
River State Hospital—you had to go down
hallways with empty tall windows and rows
and rows of skinny white skinned white gowned
white eyed mumbling reaching women
who all wanted just to touch a child–hands—
those hands–my mother and grandmother
walking fast in front–you had to count
the rows of beds and then the number in
from the side—Fifty hundred hundred fifty
mothers bare-backed bone thin gray white
gowns. We untied her hands, pressed in them
a few strings of licorice. She put it to her
empty mouth. Lips stained, mouth running
black. "She hides it," the nurses scold
and take it away. "It makes a mess." Sticky.
Sweet. Mess.

The Sweetest Water in the World

came from a pump to a wooden trough
and a simple dipper just below the fire
tower on Belknap Mountain. It was a hike
the kids could make with dads after dinner
on a summer's evening, a rush up the red
trail and those who needed, or cared, to go
slow could take the kinder gentler meandering
green. Everyone ran down the red. By spring
it was a rock river fed by that same sweet
well, that same snow deep locked in rock
and root and thick rich moss kept safe to cool
our child hot necks and cheeks before
the last climb, the knock on the floor
of the watcher's keep—glass lifted still higher
than the mountain rock's wind cleared view.

Swing

for Ed & Esther Galing
Frank & Helen Hickey
Joyce & Joe Jiudice
Kay and Jack Kelly

He cradles her, naked, in his arms, his
beautiful Fran, tight fists pounding his chest,
legs flailing; he tests the water with his
elbow, lowers her in; his hands caress

her lips, try to still the curses spitting
from her once devout tongue, and she quiets,
long enough to let him scrub the feces
off her hips, her thighs; he whispers darling,

wraps her in towels warm from the drier,
brushes her hair, clips it out of her eyes
with a child's barrette; he is the sailor
in the mirror, she is the hurried bride

mother of six children, grandmother
to eighteen. He's never kissed another.

She struggles, refuses the bra, barely
tolerates the humiliation of
Depends; he quickly wraps the only soft
old dress she'll accept, zips it, narrowly

escaping the saliva that dribbles
down her chin; he lifts her to her feet, flips
on the old stereo, quickly fiddles
with the albums, and Benny Goodman slips

from his sleeve, her knees buckle, head thrown back,
and they're dancing, Jim and Fran Casey back
at the Roosevelt ballroom, he's on leave,
damn, she's pretty, smart, stylish, who'd believe

a big dumb guy like him'd have a chance;
but he was some dancer, and can they dance!

Tatting

(lace cap hydrangea)

what we sing in white
breathes beyond green
that the young dance with arms outflung
and the old pull in pale wings, thicken,
tighten, spit their sour joy
on the heads of pins—thread wound
to a yellowing pearl
that drops secret
beneath tired flutter
waits
a pattern sealed inside

To Late Afternoon Light

For just this moment light sheathes each bare
branch of sumac and maple, each twig
of dry weed and stick, each rusted gate,
each barbed wire tier, each cinder block;
gold light marches past, a calm dumb clock
shifting minutes through each season, late
afternoon finds its gilded clothing
warming nightfall, gentling everywhere
the broken, trailing, torn off pieces
of man and nature, the cast-off things
past usefulness, upon those faceless
belongings and beginnings, light clings–
the quiet blessing of four o'clock
for things as they are, as we are not.

Tumblehome

Undertaken as worthwhile project: this time of my father's
dying: muscles atrophied: nerve broken: skin bruised
and failing healing: and I: near forty: a woman abandoned:
come home with three small children: to choose the right canoe:
to carry us over flat water: Salt Marsh Pond: the wide Saco
River: brown warm ooze: the Pine Barrens: evenings
we studied catalogs: searched want ads to find the right vessel:
he taught me what to look for: length of course: we must
seat four: mother: three: six: eight year old: each child could
choose a paddle: beam wide: for greater stability: depth:
for carrying capacity: keel: in case of cross-wind: knife-like
entry: efficiency: symmetry: versatility: shallow arch bottom:
all-around performance: moderate rocker (the curve of the keel
line from bow to stern): compromise maneuverability with
good tracking: plan made: ideal unfound: children grown:
his ashes buried in pine: the last canoe awaits me on a trestle:
fiberglass skinned: the final most important variable: weight
32 pounds: strength failed he could lift it to the top of the car
alone: and mysterious ungraspable tumblehome: the cup:
the curve: the bowl to: narrower beam at the gunwales: yielding:
ease for the paddler: home

Tune

My father never sang to me.
My mother did. Not words.
My mind keeps the murmur,
metronome enduring counting
my days. It is the song carried
over the back of the car seat,
lines swallowed by wind
and the movement of wheels,
song carried from mountain,
down hill by valley, by river.
The words are a heartbeat,
a breath, and a sigh. I sing it
alone. I sing it in silence.
My voice carries the stone.

Twilight

he sun was bright on the snow this afternoon.
Three times this week we began the day with
the blessing of an inch on twigs and branches.

It is good to have the sad dirt of the city covered.
Driving is hard but if I remember to open my eyes
I cannot curse such beauty. Now that I am older

it is the late light of afternoon I value most. That thin
gold light, holy, but hinting of endings. How many
times did you and I push off into a setting sun?

I imagine the children are good skiers now, they've
gone with their father's family each winter. But I
have heard they are not as good as I was. I had

the best teacher. I remember how you teased me:
you said I didn't really become good until I started
skiing with boys. That required that I accept

a certain reckless edge. You never asked that of me.
You would be so proud of the children now. Kate
works so hard and seriously but is still full of joy

about life. Jamie has really hit his stride this year,
doing steady work and taking responsibility. He is
taller than both sisters now. And Jenny, well

Jenny is at that age of reckless skiing. She went
to the Poconos last weekend with two boys. Now
the really reckless ones go snowboarding. Things

change. We miss you. I realize the children never
skied with you or even went fishing. Somehow
they never got the chance. We were always so busy

and your legs were doing poorly these last years,
and then your heart. Kate dreamed that you took
them fishing. I thought about rowing the great rowboat,

the heavy oars crossing above my lap, sun gone
past setting. Silence. In the dream, Kate said,
you caught only little fish. She said they were caught

without hooks or poles. They just came into your
hands for a moment, leaping silver, came,
were held, glimmered, and then you let them go.

Union

Congregations of gnats dance
intricate figures suspended just
above my head. The sun cools
behind a cloud, winds shift;
they dip toward me—my face,
my hair, my breath, now part
of their universe. The sun
shows; they rise. I am left within
the memory of their song
singing through the wires
of my electric body, my mind.

Valley Green

There shall be an opening
through which this life
shall flow

I have always been this woman
walking through woods
alone. Now I face
the limitations of my love.
I have refused the gifts
within myself.

Lead me to mass.
I shall weep again
It is no fault to seek god
again and again
in a single day. Is it wrong
to ask for grace?

Twice now I have been given
the gift of the deer
grazing, almost beyond seeing,
at the edge of the forest.
We must believe to find them,
in silence, waiting, cautious,
without fear.

Venie knew the names of apples

Buckingham. Gravenstein. MacIntosh. Gala.
Northern Spy. Jonathan. Empire. Rome.
In 1960 we stopped at a table in Poughkeepsie's
downtown department store. It was a famous name,
one you'd know, if you grew up there, one of those
places with a soda fountain and a cafeteria
in the basement, owned by some important family,
with cool marble slabs for making chocolates
and a milliner's and a hairdresser and a counter
where they'd mix face powder just for your
complexion from a row of multi-colored jars.
Pippin. Queen. Delicious. Tulpehocken.
Winesap. Granny Smith. Smokehouse. Braeburn.
It was a fall contest, harvest, back to school.
I watched my grandmother pick up each apple, inhale,
roll its skin against her cheek and forehead, pronounce
names I never learned, local varieties, each with a season
and a purpose, this the butcher's daughter knew.
King David. Spitzenberg. Campfield. Stayman.
Black Gilliflower. Bottle Greening. Cortland. Pie.

Waking to the calliope, waking to the town

band warming up across the street, Old Home
Day, and it's all sunlight, the birds are pushing
with joy to rival all our greetings—Oh, sweet running
down the stairs, chairs set out for the crowds expected,
friends returning, remembering: such a full
day, and so much lost. Doc's children gathered

under my sugar maple. Sandy holds Gabriel, gathered
up, in the crook of her arm. Nine days old, home
six days, you can already see the red in his hair, full
sunlight catching his mother's flaming ponytail, pushing
her other children in the stroller. The parade's expected
any moment now. First the police chief, kids running

alongside, and lots of laughing, more kids running
for the candy the politicians throw. Odd, we're gathered
on the lawn talking about cadavers. Who would have expected
Doc, and now Ginnie, his wife, Sandy's mother, home
alone a year then gone. Last year Sam was pushing
her in the wheelchair but she still had a full

life—friends, family, active in town affairs, a full
calendar every week. Who'd have thought she'd stop running
for office? Why just last winter she was pushing
for funds for the new library. The bond failed. I gathered
she took that hard. She'd loved work so. Sam, come home
to stay with her, Alex too, we never expected

the heart attack that came to him so young, unexpected,
before his mother's death, and Sandy, a grandmother full
six times to my none. Her work is hospice—home,
my green lawn's full of children but my own are running
further off, gone; there will be fireworks, people gathered—
I'll find a child to laugh into my mother's ear. She's pushing

eighty. She didn't ask to hold Sandy's grandson, not pushing,
but she wishes she had a great-grand, that's expected,
and how odd to think of Doc's descendents gathered
today that will never meet him. And his last students—full
year of anatomy—a donated cadaver—did he leave a running
joke behind—a swallowed coin, a wooden tooth, home

sweet home tattoo to push the medical students to learn
something unexpected, beyond muscle and bone, a running gag,
a full good laugh. Where does laughter live? We're gathered.

Was long time waitress

43 years
she knew our orders
before we took off our coats
brought the coffee
iced tea in season
asked about the children
knew their names and hobbies
but we always had
to re-read her nametag
and only reading
the paper today
do I know she had
a son

Weeding

I didn't plan this garden. Working
methodically, ten feet a day, I can
weed it all in a summer and then
start again. As I pull things away
I open continual signs of purpose:
thyme spilling over stones, its
scent in praise of every footstep;
insistent fierce stalks of duckweed
calling hummingbirds; sumac scouts
hiding in the milkweed, (saved for
monarchs and cocoons.) I make
my own shade, working at dusk. I stay
careful, away from the woodchuck's
insistently re-opened door, the hidden
yellow jacket hive, the shiver of a snake
skin glinting on stone. I cut back
spent blossoms, transplant a wildflower
into the ordered field. I use my bare
hands, fingers a part of this earth.
The skunk brushes against my leg.
He blesses me with his scentless
presence and goes out into his night.

What would we do without mourning

doves? That pair on Winnie's doorstep
that took flight the moment we opened
the door, their sound like an ascending
crystal whirlwind, a whinnying brook,
a book read with pages of metal
turning on their own—it's spring but
the ground is still covered with at least
ten inches of snow, and they're pecking
and moving their heads like Egyptians
come alive on the side of a tomb. Winnie
is happy to feed them. She's forgetful,
she's lonely, confused. They remind her
she once had a husband. And it's spring.
She wasn't always alone.

Wild Root Charlie

lived on the Cat Path. Employed by the Fish
and Game department to test fences he had
a wife and a fawn and an appetite for cigarettes.
Daddy'd take me after supper bump dusting
down the narrow road and we'd click our tongues
at the turn-around 'til Charlie'd come nosing
his smooth cool face through the wire's diamonds
to tongue my carefully offered carrot and potato
peel. I longed for the doe who stood
at the edge of the trees and the tiny face peeking
beneath her flank. Oh, Charlie. One day you leapt
them all, seven fences, barb-wired and rolled,
picketed and spiked, storm and stockade and
electric buzz for some apple orchard in your
dreams. They retired the project. In a decade I'd
wrestle boys at the empty turn-around, their
tobacco mouths hard against my teeth, remember
your beauty and grace and wonder did your doe
still wait out in that darkness for your return.

Winnipesaukee/Summer

Temporary encampment—
women and children
shaken on the sand;
tribes gathered, time unremembered:
the death journey
of salmon.

A mallard female pokes
her honest face
beneath my table,
her mate is molting,
emerald neck eroded,
white pinfeathers stuck at
odd tail angles.

A bone white boy passes,
his fingers pointed guns.

A woman watches my children,
dark sleek heads and cool brown
skin: What is your tribe? she asks.
None. We are imposters,
bastards, mongrels, families forgotten,
tribes chased away centuries ago.
We sift old bones in our buckets,
shell, fish, bird, man.

Without a clue

My mother said, we lost him, as if he were
the car keys, as if he were a lucky penny fallen
between the cushions of the couch, as if he'd wandered
off at dawn in his night shirt with frazzled hair
looking for a place to hide and sneak
a cigarette and even now men were beating
the bushes from Hatch Drive
to Wilson's field calling; as if he'd left us
for some mistress, some other family he'd kept
secret 'til this morning when they needed him
more than we did, his body gone already
to the morgue—vanished, not a finger
print left on the door knob, not a single white
hair, lost, like a losing hand
at poker, like a button popped
from a vest, like a missing pair of cuff-links,
like one mitten in a pair and I'd have to keep
the other hand in my pocket all winter, lost,
like his eagle scout badge I dropped
somewhere on the mountain, lost,
as if he were the dog coaxed away
with a marrow bone, as if you were a bad bet, she says
you're lost, lost, as if she'd stapled fliers
to telephone poles, left them at the supermarket,
where even now people are tearing off
the little slips with our phone number
and any day now will be calling with good news.

Yankees

You call, concerned the recent snowfall will aggravate
the already serious risk of roof collapse.
You intend to avoid further damage,
wishing, as always, that I avoid expense, force me frugal
in these, my foolish endeavors. I thank you for your support,
tense fingers tapping the counter, I must sustain

amity between us, this awkward role, sustain
us as adult-adult, not let the parent-child role aggravate
the effect of what I know is intended simple clean support,
still, I hear judgement, hints at catastrophes beyond the collapse
of mere old houses, your words kept tight, frugal
emotion held, opinion unexpressed respecting damage

already dealt, that pain a parent holds, damage
we are helpless to keep our children from, even less can we sustain
them in the slow return from dark, no, use words frugal
in the silence of love, as if by loving too much we might aggra-
vate
the loss of other loves, tip our children's hearts into collapse.
We keep closed hands, crossed arms, strong, withdraw support

as if that were a blessing, as if support
given those we love necessarily brings damage
to their budding separate achievements which must collapse
beneath a helping parent hand, fail to sustain
young confidence: a moment's lapse toward care might aggravate
hid tendencies toward weakness. Oh, keep frugal

love, a Yankee heart, doors locked against the rain, more frugal
than might even hint at the extravagant support
we want to give. It is a house, not my life. Don't aggravate
my loss of competence. Don't speak of building flaws and
damage
when it's my choices you wish to repair. I can't sustain
my self-respect against that vision. I fight collapse

every day, every hour. I read it in your pauses, the collapse
of hope, and I hold back, too, speak frugal
to your wanting heart. I have inherited the need to sustain
this myth between us, that neither of us needs the other's support,
that neither of us has suffered any damage,
not bereavement, not failure; we do not speak of sorrow, lest we aggravate
the other's broken heart, collapse the fiction. We support
by locked up silence, frugal love, lie safety, blind damage
love that might sustain our injured, wounded, we aggravate our
loss.

The Year Turning

December 31st. Boy trudging heavy boots toward the hollow, gun on his back. I hear the shot. Shots. I've been hearing them all weekend. Odd. I've left the city street violence for this quiet dirtroad peace. I've come for silence. Four shots yesterday. I turn away from the window. You answer the agitated knock. He's hit something. The deer didn't go down. He tried for a finishing shot. Missed. Now he's lost the blood trail. You go out with the dog. Soon an uncle and a cousin, you're four silhouetted on the ridge. You come back red and breathless. Fire up the stove. He must have winged it. Never found it. You say people round here are good with guns. I worry. Remember three boys shot in my high school alone. Boy's back on the first. Angry. There's a deer left dead by the abandoned homestead. Across the road. Bloated. 'Bout three days dead. You talk about the angle of the shot, up through the shoulder. How he found the bullet in the small tree behind, kneehigh. No blood path. No confusion. No run. A sinful waste. The boy's outraged. Meat gone bad. His father's dying. You told me that before we slept last night, before you let the fire burn down. He's a good kid. Quiet. Responsible. Safe. I'm barefoot in the slush of the kitchen yard. Thinking about another boy.
Talking about bear. This boy tells me a bear once scratched on the door to the trailer. That doublewide, just down the road. His dad grew up there. He's 37. A tumor. Can't say what kind. Cousins and uncles take the boy out shooting. Or he goes alone. Hunting season ended at midnight. Never found his deer.

Yellow Jacket

the whole of him throbs
wings beat hummingbird quick
pointed abdomen dab dab dabs
slower pulses
more surprising for the danger
watched he beats
exultation in a blush of melon
juice like a kitten lapping milk
like a dog gulping water after
a long walk that tap tap tap
quick time tap feeler twitch
then the forelegs climb
the mountain of a peach
fall back stunned spent
too much to miracle too much
beckoning sweet I tip him into
grass unstuck he flies in circles
dazzled, lost

The 400,000

This year my mother went alone.
She set up her lawn chair at McIntyre Circle
just where the road was closed to automobile
traffic, watched the parade lead by Peter Fonda
and Evil Knievel's son. Seventy-five. Same
age as the rally and the Gypsy Motor Tour.

When I was a kid my dad would take me
to the basement of the fire station
to see all the impounded bikes.
In those days the road came right by
the Village Store. Big beer business.
State Troopers must have made the arrests.

We didn't have but a police chief and Tim
Landroche's dad as part-time cop.
My parents used to go up to the Belknap
and sit with the other volunteer firemen
on the truck and wait for the drag racers
to catch on fire. That's what they did.

Some of the locals tried it too. They'd lay
down two stripes of gasoline, light 'em,
and try to race the fire down the middle.
I saw the real races too. Winding, screaming
around the roads at the campsites. We made
my deaf grandmother stand right at the fence.

Just about blew her over when they came.
They called it off in '63 and I think that was
the year of the riot. Our very own motorcycle riot.
We'd driven through a few hours before. I'd held
my new kitten up to the window to wave,
a VW bug. A few hours later they were burning cars.

The National Guard couldn't get into Weirs Beach,
that narrow road. The bikes just took the hill climbs fast
out. I'm not sure how they decided to start the races
again. Sled dogs and motorcycles. That's what
Laconia had, and it was a musher built the racetrack.
Seats about 100,000. Mostly they use if for Nascar

but they built it for motorcycles. Hell's Angels
bought land nearby cause nobody wanted
to rent to them. I haven't been up there
much since high school, but I did go in '87
when my mother had her second heart attack.

Took my baby son. She was mad cause
they'd kicked her out of the ICU to make room–
all the "motor vehicle" accidents and shootings
and fights and overdoses and the occasional
guy that blew himself up playing with a grenade–

She wanted to see the show, maybe park
a wheelchair down in the ER. Her doctors said no.
But we took her sister and sat in the parking lot
at McDonald's to watch it go by. About forty
roared into the space beside us and a guy walked over,

leather leather, muscle muscle, bald head
like the Humungus in Road Warrior, tapped on the window—
I was too shook not to roll it down:
"J'espere qu'on n'a pas reveille le bebe."
I'd forgotten how many come from Quebec.

Fin

I step out into
a sky so blue you could lean
your back against it.

Made in the USA
Middletown, DE
20 April 2021